100 TOP INTERNET JOB SITES

Books in the CAREERSAVVY Series™:

100 Top Internet Job Sites

Get Wired, Get Hired
in Today's New Job Market

Kristina M. Ackley

IMPACT PUBLICATIONS
Manassas Park, Virginia

Library of Congress Cataloging-in-Publication Data

Ackley, Kristina, 1969—
   100 top internet job sites: get wired, get hired in today's new job
   market / Kristina Ackley.
      p. cm.—(The career savvy series)
   Includes index.
   ISBN 1-57023-128-1 (alk. paper)
      1. Job hunting—Computer network resources. 2. Vocational guid-
   ance—Computer network resources. 3. Career development—
   Computer network resources. 4. Internet (Computer network) I. Title:
   One hundred top internet job sites. II. Title. III. Series

HF5382.7 .A25 2000
025.06'65014—dc21   99-089877

Publisher: For information on Impact Publications, including current and forthcoming publications, authors, press kits, bookstore, and submission requirements, visit Impact's Web site: *www.impactpublications.com*

Publicity/Rights: For information on publicity, author interviews, and subsidiary rights, contact the Public Relations and Marketing Department: Tel. 703/361-7300 or Fax 703/335-9486.

Sales/Distribution: Bookstore sales are handled through Impact's trade distributor: National Book Network, 15200 NBN Way, Blue Ridge Summit, PA 17214, Tel. 1-800-462-6420. All other sales and distribution inquiries should be directed to the publisher: Sales Department, IMPACT PUBLICATIONS, 9104 Manassas Dr., Suite N, Manassas Park, VA 20111-5211, Tel. 703/361-7300, Fax 703/335-9486, or *careersavvy@impactpublications.com*

Book design by Kristina Ackley

Contents

PREFACE

I n the summer of 1985, my father bought our family's first modem. Later that summer, with the help of a friend, I logged on to my first bulletin board system (BBS). After only a few months, I had developed the alias, "Slow Turtle" for myself, and spent much of my time typing to friends with aliases like "Spirit Walker," "Commander Diode," "Cosmic Charlie," and "Caveman."

Over the next nine years, I sporadically used BBSes to communicate with friends around the world. In graduate school, however, my online needs changed. I began using the Internet, especially email and the World Wide Web, to conduct research. Not only was I able to search online databases for immediate answers to my questions, I was also able to conduct original research and interview many diverse research subjects... without spending a dime.

When funding for my graduate assistantship ended, I needed to begin a job search. In 1995, online job-posting resources like CareerMosaic and DICE were just starting to gain popularity, but listservs and newsgroups had been widely available since the 1980s.

I posted my resume on a newsgroup called dcjobs and crossed my fingers. The Internet was still dominated by computer professionals, and many of the job leads generated from the newsgroup focused too heavily on computer programming for my interest. After a few days, I received an interesting email from the president of a small company. After a brief email exchange, an in-depth telephone interview, and a face-to-face interview, I started my new job as a government contractor.

Since my first foray into online job searching, the process has greatly expanded and improved. I again turned to the Internet for a 1996 job search. Although some of the resume posting sites offered interesting results, the *Washington Post* classifieds (the online search option was so much easier than scanning newsprint!) yielded the job I accepted. In 1998, I fully appreciated the usefulness in my job search. Not only did it enable me to more effectively search for a new job, it also provided the tools to research that company and its competitors, the salaries for my field, the status of the industry, and much more! One day, a great job found me, based on a resume I had posted to CareerWeb. After a brief telephone interview and two face-to-face interviews, I landed a fantastic job!

> **BBS (Bulletin Board System)**— free-standing computers, which provide electronic message databases where people can log in and leave messages. Messages are organized by topic groups, similar to newsgroups. Any user may submit or read messages in public areas.

At the completion of this book, I have just made another great career move, thanks to the help of Monster.com. While researching sites and job searching strategies for this book, I updated my resume and posted it online. In a couple of months, without any extra effort on my part, I received an offer to interview that I couldn't refuse. I used the Internet to research the company, the field, and the salary and benefit ranges. The Internet helped me land the job.

I started my online adventure over 15 years ago. Soon after, I added a few more to my list of numbers to call. Eventually, I established a network of communications to reach out to people across the Washington, D.C. area. Over the past few years, I have watched that network expand dramatically. I have started and managed an international networking listserv for public relations professionals in the publishing industry, and participate in at least six other listservs related to my professional development and interests.

I am consistently amazed by the growth and outreach available through the Internet. Inexperienced jobseekers can join or volunteer with a virtual organization in order to gain more experience. You can gain advice about your current career and a dream job in a completely different career area. You can make contacts around the world, post your resume for millions of potential employers to see, find a job anywhere in the world...without ever leaving your home or paying any more than the cost of a computer and an Internet account.

Get wired, get hired in today's new job market.

For Mom and Dad
for years of encouragement,
no matter how off beat I may have seemed

and to Steve
for never giving up

100 TOP INTERNET JOB SITES

1

BASIC STEPS TO LOGGING IN AND FINDING A JOB ONLINE

You've decided to search for a new job. Whether this is your first or fifteenth job search, the rules have probably changed. More and more job seekers venture beyond the traditional means of finding jobs and now include the Internet in their job search. And the online rules for job searching are different than the off-line rules.

The Internet provides a vast amount of resources previously unavailable to many job seekers. Now, in addition to browsing through newspaper classifieds, you can use many tools previously available only to headhunters and recruiters. If you stay on top of the online trends, you can make your job search free, easy, and extremely effective.

Perhaps you've used the Internet before for a job search. Or, maybe this is your first venture online and you have no idea where to start. Turn on your printer, grab your mouse, and get ready to find out about the top 100 Internet Job sites. That's what this book is all about!

Internet Origins

If you are new to computers and/or to the Internet, a brief background will help you understand cyberspace. In 1969, United States Department of Defense's Advanced Research Projects Agency (ARPA), established the first four computer sites for the Internet, then named ARPANET. Through dedicated, high-speed lines, the four computers transferred data to each other. Throughout the 70s, the network grew, and was primarily used by researchers for news and project collaboration. In 1984, the National Science Foundation (NSF) added the NFSNET to the communications process, greatly enhancing the speed and capabilities of the network. In 1989, ARPANet stepped away from the action, and the National Science Foundation (NSF) assumed responsibility for the Internet backbone. In March 1989, Tim Berners-Lee of CERN (Conseil Européen pour la Recherche Nucleaire), proposed a new communications tool for members of the widely-spread organization. The result was the World Wide Web, a subset of the Internet, a hyperlinked collection of individual pages that are accessed via Internet protocols (URLs) and interpreted through coding languages, such as HTML. Web browsers, such as Netscape and Internet Explorer, translate the language and the links so that users can easily navigate between different pages. In 1995, the NSF turned the management process over to a consortium of commercial Internet Service Providers (ISPs), and the Internet was developed into its current form.

> URL—Universal Resource Locator... the Internet address for a Web site.
>
> HTML—HyperText Markup Language... the coding language through which Web sites are created.

Connecting for the First Time

To connect to the Internet, there are several pieces of equipment you must acquire. A complete (new, but low-end) system, including monitor, printer, and computer with modem, can be purchased for approximately $500-$800. If you cannot afford this, other options for connecting to the Internet include work (which is not a good option for job searching), a cybercafe, or a nearby library or college.

If you purchase a computer, there are some options you should add in order to connect to the Internet, regardless of whether you purchase a PC or Macintosh. Your friendly computer store salesperson will provide you with plenty of confusing options, so take a little knowledge to the store with you. If you seek more in depth information, several books and magazines will prove helpful:

- *The Complete Idiot's Guide to PCs* by Joe Kraynak
- *Buying A Computer For Dummies®* by Dan Gookin
- *PCs For Dummies®* by Dan Gookin
- *Macs® For Dummies®* by David Pogue
- *How to Buy a Computer : And a Monitor, a Printer, a Sound Card, a Scanner, Etc...* by Myles White
- *ComputerShopper* magazine
- *PCWorld* magazine
- *MacWorld* magazine
- *FamilyPC* magazine

Please keep in mind that information about computer "standards" may be obsolete a week after you purchase a book. However, if you don't need the fastest, most technologically-advanced machine ever made, you'll gain more than enough information from print materials.

In order to connect to the Internet, your computer should include the following:

- **CPU** (central processing unit—the actual computer)—Some baseline standards include: Pentium 300 processor or equivalent (Celerons and K2s are also sufficient), 4MB video card, 56K modem (see below), sound card (some Internet sound is important!), 4.3 GB or higher hard drive and 32 MB RAM (Random Access Memory).

◆ **Monitor**—most computers come with a 15" monitor; many now come with a 17" monitor. The bigger the monitor, the more you can see at once. Monitor quality is determined by dots per inch, and the smaller the number (.27 is pretty standard), the sharper the images.

◆ **Modem**—the device that translates digital information into your computer. The current standard is a 56 Kbps modem, but you can also connect to the Internet via cable modems, ISDN, T-lines, and a variety of other methods. The faster the speed, the more quickly Web sites will open for you.

◆ **Printer**—not mandatory, but you'll quickly discover the advantages of owning a printer. InkJet printers are lower cost ($100-$300), but also lower quality. Laser printers, though higher quality, can be prohibitively expensive.

◆ **Software**—word processing program (WordPerfect and Microsoft Word are two industry standards) and Internet browser/email program (Netscape or Internet Explorer should be included with your computer). The word processing program will help you create quality resumes and cover letters; the browser/email program will enable you to view Web pages and read and respond to email.

You will also need to sign up with an Internet Service Provider (ISP). ISPs provide a way for your modem to connect to the Internet with a high-speed link. The most important consideration in choosing an ISP is finding one that provides a local phone number for you to dial, or you will quickly start accruing long distance charges! Many computers will come with free trials from national ISPs, such as America OnLine. You can also contact ISPs.com, which provides comprehensive information on over 4,000 Internet Service Providers in the United States and Canada, including pricing and service areas...or check your local newspaper or phone book. When you contact an ISP, make sure they provide at least 56k connection speeds, an email account for you to send and receive electronic mail, and access to Internet newsgroups. Other factors that may affect your decision include the modem to user ratio, the cost (under $19.95 per month is reasonable), and the years the ISP has been in business. Your ISP will provide instructions for connecting to the Internet using their services; each company varies in its specifics.

Preparing for Success in Cyberspace

If you can connect to the Internet, you're already ahead of a significant number of job searchers. Despite its amazing growth and potential, the Internet still only reaches about 25% of the US population and 38% of the Canadian population. That means that 75% of Americans and 62% of Canadians do not have the same advantage as you... conducting a job search via the Internet! The Internet need not be the end-all, be all, in your job search; but it does show that you have more initiative than "the unconnected" in preparing yourself for the future! Where else can you find free networking events, places to post your resume, international job opportunities, resources through which to research companies in which you are interested, and 24-hour availability?

If you are a novice to the Internet, you will discover so many resources available to make your early visits to cyberspace less intimidating and confusing. Visit local computer stores, such as CompUSA, for information on training courses. Consider special on-site training programs like New Horizons and CareerTrack. Many community colleges offer introductory courses for new users. Try to sign up for hands-on, interactive classes.

If you prefer to work in the privacy of your own home or office, you can pick from a number of useful, hands-on training courses:

Internet Training Videos and CD-ROMS

- *How to Understand, Access, and Use the Internet* (Video)
  CareerTrack, (800) 488-0928
- *Discover the Internet* (Video)
  Video Tutor, (800) 790-9120
- *Internet Training CD-ROM Tutorial*
  Charles River Media, (800) 382-8505
- *Using the Internet with Windows 98* (CD-ROM)
  PC Connection, (888) 213-0260

Books

- *The Internet for Dummies* (6th Ed), by John R. Levine, Carol Baroudi, Margaret Levine Young
- *Dummies 101®: The Internet For Windows® 98*, by Hy Bender, Margaret Levine Young
- *How the Internet Works, Millennium Edition,* by Preston Gralla
- *The Complete Idiot's Guide to the Internet* (6th Ed), by Peter Kent

For a small fee, www.CompUsa.com, www.learn2.com, www.trainingontheweb.net, and www.smartplanet.com offer online courses to familiarize beginners with using the Internet or Internet applications. If you need really quick, free help, www.learnthenet.com provides a great tutorial.

A Word About Netiquette

Those entering the culture of the Internet should familiarize them-selves with online etiquette, also known as "netiquette." These con-ventions are not clearly defined; time provides the best examples for Internet users to follow. Netiquette includes the proper use of capi-talization, proper methods of marketing (as opposed to bulk emailing, or "spamming"), and ensuring that messages pertain to the current discussion. Users who intend to employ the Internet as a business tool must acquaint themselves with this knowledge quickly. Without this information, they will encounter little respect or tolerance from vet-eran users. If you are attempting to show prospective employers your technology savvy, you need to learn how to act appropriately.

Top Ten DO's and DON'Ts for Net Surfing

1. **DON'T** include in a mail message anything you wouldn't put on a Times Square billboard.
2. **DON'T** send chain letters. They're obnoxious, they waste valuable time and space, and your ISP may delete your account as a result.
3. **DON'T** pass on information about viruses **unless** you have first checked to make sure they are not hoaxes (urbanlegends.about.com is a great resource!).
4. **DON'T** send large amounts of unsolicited information/ bulk email ("SPAM") to people. You may lose your ac-count as a result of this action.
5. **DON'T** flame. Flaming is strongly criticizing or "picking a fight" with another user.
6. **DO** follow the same ethics and legal guidelines you ob-serve off the Net. Plagiarism, pornography, and slamming are still plagiarism, pornography, and slamming—online.

7. **DO** keep confidences. Do not quote a personal letter in a posting to a group of people without first requesting permission from the original sender.
8. **DO** respect others' right to privacy, and do not pester them for personal information such as sex, age, or location.
9. **DO** use a combination of upper and lower case. TYPING IN ALL CAPS IS CONSIDERED "SHOUTING."
10. **DO** keep signature files (automatic identifiers at the end of a message) and emoticons (smilies) to a minimum!

Search...and You Will Find Anything

Search engines provide valuable help to everyone, from the newest novice to the most experienced Internet user. They search the Internet for results in a variety of different manners, from accepting questions to specially-formatted keywords and combinations. They provide a base from which you can start for jobs, either through special links or by using keyword searches for job titles!

Search engines can be a bit tricky for the uninitiated, but with a little practice, you can find anything online. The first step is to choose which words you want to look up. For this introductory search, we'll be looking for jobs for Web site designers. The second step is to determine the search engine's protocol for searches. Some search engines require users to use "and," "or," and "not" to identify how to search. Others use + or - to distinguish which words to include in your search. Many search engines accept both formats, and most enable you to search for phrases by enclosing the text in quotes. All of them should have a clearly identifiable area for more help on the best way to search on that engine. You can play around with a variety of combinations for your search, depending on the search engine, such as:

"jobs for Web site designers"

+jobs +Web +site +designers

jobs and Web and site and designers

+jobs +"Web site designers"

Note: Certain words, such as "Web" and "Internet" appear so prevalently on the Internet that the search engine may refuse to search for them, or will notify you that an exorbitant number of results exists for that particular word. Searching for "Web" produced over 24 million results on AllTheWeb, 115 million on AltaVista, and 21.4 million on Infoseek. Searching for +job +"web site designer" on these sites, however, produced 1,415 results on AllTheWeb, 1,800 on AltaVista, and 91 on Infoseek. Narrowing your search definitely produces more manageable results.

Over the past few years, the number of search engines has grown dramatically, but the following ten sites should provide quick and thorough ways to meet your job searching needs...and then some:

All the Web	Search Engine
www.alltheweb.com	

Extremely fast in returning results. Very simple format without distracting bells and whistles. Has teamed up with Lycos (another popular search engine) to enable users to search for a specific file. AllTheWeb is conducting "The World's Biggest Search—The Quest for One Billion URLs." Also includes job opportunities within FAST, the company that owns All the Web.

AltaVista	Search Engine
www.altavista.com	

Users may search the Web, news, or discussions for their desired topics, in a variety of languages. Advanced searches include the ability to search within a specific range of dates and to show one result per Web site. Users may also browse through a variety of categories for their topic. Clicking on the "jobs" link will take you to careers.altavista.com, Alta Vista's fantastic career site!

Dogpile   Search Engine
www.dogpile.com

Cute, friendly format enables users to "fetch" their search desires, whether from the Web, Newsgroups, FTP, Yellow pages, or stock quotes. Dogpile also offers categories through which users may search for specific topics. Part of Go2Net, which also provides a search engine at www.go2net.com.

Excite   Search Engine
www.excite.com

Excite provides a total, customizable environment for Internet searchers. Although the initial view may be a bit overwhelming, the results from this dynamite search engine are worth a second look. Results are returned both as Web site links and as news articles, and searches are listed in order of relevance. Selecting the "Career" link here takes you to Excite Careers, which points you on your way to a dream job!

HotBot   Search Engine
www.hotbot.com

This bright, easy to use site will return 10, 25, 50, or 100 matches for your search. You decide how many, how recently they occurred, whether you're looking for a person, page title, or links to a page. The advanced search lets you get even more specific, including the geographic location of the page and more! The jobs link under the "business & money" section provides career advice you won't want to miss.

Infoseek	Search Engine
www.infoseek.com	

Part of the Go Network, this site lets you tailor your search to the Web, news, special topics, newsgroups, or companies. Special features include personalized start pages and a translator that enables users to translate English to or from other languages, which may be quite helpful when looking for an international job. The "Careers" link moves you into Go Careers, sponsored by CareerPath, and host to over 200,000 careers!

Northern Light	Search Engine
www.northernlight.com	

Although word and phrase searches work on Northern Light, users may also conduct "natural language" searches... the user can type in questions, such as "where can I find a Web site design job?" Searches may also be narrowed to newspapers, wires, and transcripts, or just college newspapers.

Snap	Search Engine
www.snap.com	

Freshly merged with NBC.com and Xoom.com, Snap provides a variety of resources, in a customizable setting. Advanced users can narrow their searches to include specific dates, domains, or people. Snap even offers a special option for high-speed users; select this and you'll see a variety of special, high-end features. The "Career" link takes you to a complete career center, with a variety of career links, from minority and disability career issues to resume posting sites.

WebCrawler
www.webcrawler.com
Search Engine

Powered by Excite, WebCrawler works differently than traditional search engines. It functions as a Web robot, building indices from information it automatically seeks and identifies on the Web. The site also includes WebCrawler Direct, which lets you search from your desktop with a single mouse click. It was the first full-text search engine. Click on the easily found "Career" link to see a variety of resources and job links!

Yahoo
www.yahoo.com
Search Engine

This versatile site enables users to search by either keywords or categories, and it returns search information via categories, Web sites, Web pages, related news, and Net events. Yahoo will also search Usenet for information and includes an extensive shopping area for additional resources. Users may also create a personalized page to improve their Net usage.

Several other useful sites use search functions, but extend beyond your typical search engine and deserve a special mention:

Ask Jeeves
www.ask.com
Search Engine

Untangle the mysteries of the Web in this unique environment through which you can search for information. Presenting a clever, friendly interface (with what question might the butler, Jeeves, help you?), Ask Jeeves removes the intimidation factor from the

Net by encouraging you to ask questions in simple, everyday language. Jeeves successfully answers your questions because he catalogues the answers to all questions asked, creating a type of "artificial intelligence"... with each question asked, he increases his knowledge. In addition to asking whatever questions you desire to have answered, you can see questions concurrently being asked by other users and read through some of the most popular questions. Jeeves will even show where to find the answers on some of the major search engines, such as AltaVista, Infoseek, and About.com.

| *About.com* | Search Engine |
| www.about.com | |

About.com re-humanizes the Internet experience, by providing human "guides" who help you search for information. About.com provides a simple search engine that helps you identify the area in which you would like to search, but after that point, the human guides do the rest of the work!

Over 650 highly targeted environments (including job searching!) focus on specific topics and are overseen by a knowledgeable human guide. The guides create and maintain Internet directories that include approximately 400,000 pre-screened links to other Web sites, which are summarized by the guides, enabling you to quickly find relevant Internet content. Additionally, users with like interests can form "communities" by communicating with each other directly or through the guides.

| *Webopedia* | Search Engine |
| webopedia.internet.com | |

Isn't Java a type of coffee? What exactly is TCP/IP, and do you need to learn it? Do you have protocol? If you're confused about any of these questions, Webopedia most likely can help. Providing a simple, easily understood interface and definitions for computer and Internet terms that every technophobe can understand, this site will prove invaluable as you search for answers to your questions.

How This Book Helps You Find a Job Online

Now that you've figured out how to search for the answers to all of your questions, you're ready to start looking for a job online. You can use the search engines to search for jobs which include keywords relevant to your skills and experience. You will not, however, utilize the full potential of the Internet unless you tailor and expand your search.

The chapters in this book are carefully organized to walk you through the online job search process, from self-assessment to following-up on your applications:

Chapter 2—Assess your career options, through exploration of your interests and experiences. Learn more about different careers, through professional associations and online networking.

Chapter 3—Put your best face forward by learning how to successfully prepare resumes and cover letters. Prepare to ace interviews and land your dream job.

Chapter 4—Find jobs, consulting opportunities, and recruiters online. Post your resume to top job search sites and be recognized by the top employers.

Chapter 5—Research, research, research. Before you contact an employer, you need to know more about them and their industry. Learn where to go online to get the hottest information about the organizations, their competition, and industry forecasts and trends.

Chapter 6—Wrap it up. Prepare for the interview by researching the trends and statistics for your chosen career. Learn the salary ranges for your career level and location. Determine the benefits for which you should bargain. Also learn the real cost of relocation.

Why did I rank the sites in this book in the top 100? I have carefully researched these and other sites, and these sites clearly met the following criteria:

- ◆ **Ease of use**—the site must be easy to navigate; spending hours learning how to use a site won't help you on a job search. Graphic appeal was also a consideration for this category; nobody likes an ugly site!

- ◆ **Cost**—in most cases, free, but several exemplary, fee-based services have been added to the list.

- ◆ **Timeliness and quality of information**—out-of-date and inaccurate information will hinder, rather than help, your job search process. The reviewed sites stay on top of the trends and issues you need to know.

- ◆ **Effectiveness**—quality, not quantity. All of the information in the world won't help you unless the information is effective in satisfying your needs. These sites meet, and often surpass, their basic goals.

The best part of using the Internet is that you can have fun. Keep this in mind while you're searching for a job. The opportunities are endless, and the market is ripe for qualified job seekers.

2

FINDING YOUR DREAM CAREER

Now that you're familiar with using the Internet, how do you know which career you want to pursue? Have you identified your dream career, or are you completely clueless when it comes to a career search? Do you truly know which career is best for you? The Internet provides a variety of online tools to help you consider numerous alternatives.

By taking a few minutes to answer questions on a self-assessment test, you will not only narrow down some career possibilities and alternatives that match your interests, but you will also better prepare yourself for a chosen career. Especially if the career represents new skills and ideas with which you are not familiar, increasing your knowledge of the nature of the work, working conditions, and training and education necessary to excel in that career can only work to your advantage. After you have identified your dream career and reviewed some of the standard job descriptions, it's time to delve deeper into the profession in which you are interested. A variety of networking opportunities exist online, from associations to listservs. The information provided there may prove highly beneficial to you in a job interview, as it demonstrates your awareness of the challenges you may encounter.

The resources in this chapter explore self-assessment tools, professional associations, and networking opportunities available for different careers. Many of the sites will identify education and professional affiliations that may help you excel in certain career fields. They also suggest related occupations and general outlooks for the career fields, as well as resources for additional information. This chapter does not identify specific jobs available within the career fields or information about individual companies within different career sectors; these topics will be covered in Chapters 4 and 5.

Self-Assessment

Self-assessment tests will help match your interests and personality with appropriate careers, based on your unique strengths and weaknesses at the testing time. However, the results of these tests should not be used as your sole reason for career or job selection. Instead, they should be viewed as an invaluable way to explore potential career and occupational opportunities, understand your job skill strengths and challenges, and manage your current job responsibilities to avoid difficulties with your weak areas. Before you start looking for a new job, you really need to conduct a self-assessment to give more focus and substance to your job search.

The Web provides everyone with access to career tests, opening up a new dimension of job searching for many that was previously available only through career counselors. Whenever possible, I have identified top Web sites for the more popular self-assessment tests; however, due to the complexity of creating an objective testing environment, and scoring and interpreting the tests, some are not currently available online or are only available on a fee basis. With the increasing demand for online career development, these tests will become more readily available. Please bear in mind that although they are most effective when administered by a professional, the online versions can still get you started on your career search.

The main types of tests include Personality Inventories, Interest Inventories, and Aptitude/Intelligence tests. Personality tests measure how you relate in work and play situations, focusing on feelings, desires, and emotions. Interest inventories attempt to identify how you react to certain activities and what you enjoy, assuming interesting work will be more satisfying and you will be more productive. Intelligence tests measure specific aptitudes and your ability or interest in learning. Some of the more well-known tests include:

◆ Career Ability Placement Survey (CAPS)

◆ Career Assessment Inventory (CAI)

◆ Campbell Interest and Skill Survey (CISS)

◆ Edwards Personal Preference Schedule (EPPS)

◆ Holland Self-Directed Search (SDS)

◆ Inquiry Mode Questionnaire (InQ)

◆ Jackson Vocational Interest Survey (JVIS)

◆ Keirsey Character Sorter

◆ Kuder Occupational Interest Survey (KOIS)

◆ Life Styles Inventory (LSI)

◆ Myers-Briggs Type Indicator (MBTI)

◆ Personal Effectiveness Inventory (PEI)

◆ Slosson Intelligence Test (SIT-R)

◆ Strong Interest Inventory (SII)

◆ Wechsler Intelligence Scales (WAIS-R & WISC-R)

There are some limitations to conducting the tests without the help of a qualified counselor, since your answers, and therefore your interpretations, may be subjective. You may fail to critically assess your results, immediately reject your results as inaccurate, "fake" your answers to identify a career you think you want, or form biases toward the tests or careers indicated. A qualified counselor can provide proper administration, interpretation, and discussion of the results, and will also be able to select the appropriate test from the plethora of tests available. She can objectively interpret the results within the context of your life, social environment, personal history, and behavior.

A wide variety of credentials exists for career counselors. Not all credentials are the same and the requirements for attaining them can vary dramatically. To locate a certified career counselor or to learn more about their credentials, training, and qualifications, search the following organizations online:

- ◆ The National Board for Certified Counselors, Inc.— www.nbcc.org—National Certified Career Counselor (NCCC) certification

- ◆ The National Career Networking Association— www.ncna.com—Certified Career Counselor (CCC) certification

- ◆ International Association of Career Management Professionals—www.iacmp.org—Certified Practitioner (CMP), Fellow Practitioner (CMF), and Fellow Manager (CMF)

- ◆ American Counseling Association (ACA)— www.counseling.org—does not directly certify counselors, but contains a variety of useful information for counselors and individuals seeking counseling. Contains a division, the National Career Development Association (NCDA), which certifies Career Development Facilitators (CDF)

While most assessment tests are administered by trained counselors, some are also available online. The following sites present several useful self-assessment devices that you can access and use on your own.

The Holland Self-Directed Search (SDS)

Based on the theory that people are happier and more successful in jobs that match their interests, values, and skills, this test asserts that people can be loosely classified into six different groups: Realistic, Investigative, Artistic, Social, Enterprising, and Conventional (RIASEC). Most people are a blend of two or more types; few people are pure types. Knowing the extent and specific limitations of your mental abilities can allow you to accentuate the positives and compensate for the negatives in your list of abilities.

Self-Directed-Search www.self-directed-search.com	Assessment

An interactive, online test from the publishers of the SDS, Psychological Assessment Resources, Inc. Quickly breeze through the four categories: activities, competencies, occupations, and self-estimates, to gain a "feel" for the SDS, but pay $7.95 to receive your results and evaluation. The extensive report includes more details about your type, careers relevant to your type (with the *Dictionary of Occupational Titles* [*DOT*] code), education and training needed for those careers, and additional information.

The Career Key www.ncsu.edu/careerkey/career_key.html	Assessment

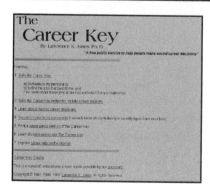

The Career Key asks you to identify which jobs interest you, what you like to do, your abilities, how you see yourself, and what you value, then compiles the results of your answers to create your career key. You then identify jobs that are interesting to you, according to the RIASEC types in which your scores are strongest. A list of applicable jobs appears, and selecting any of the jobs listed takes you directly to the *Occupational Outlook Handbook* definition for that career. The site allows you to save your results for future use.

> ### Indiana Career & Postsecondary Adv. Center   Assessment
> ### icpac.indiana.edu/infoseries/is-50.html

Providing an extremely basic feel for the SDS, this site asks you only to select subjects or activities that are most appealing to you before returning your scores and a list of possible careers. Clicking on the careers introduces the job, as well as offers worker characteristics, physical demands, work settings, wages, outlooks, preparation steps, related occupations, military specialties, education/training programs, and job openings. Some of the jobs even provide brief videos to introduce the career. The front page guides you through several interesting advising sections, including knowing your abilities, assessing your skills, determining skills you need, and prioritizing your goals.

Keirsey Character Sorter

Derived from Carl Jung's theory of "psychological types" and similar to the Myers-Briggs test, the questionnaire identifies four temperament types, which can be broken into four variants:

- **Guardians:** Supervisor ESTJ, Inspector ISTJ, Provider ESFJ, Protector ISFJ

- **Artisans:** Promoter ESTP, Operator ISTP, Performer ESFP, Composer ISFP

- **Idealists:** Teacher ENFJ, Counselor INFJ, Champion ENFP, Healer INFP

- **Rationals:** Fieldmarshal ENTJ, Mastermind INTJ, Inventor ENTP, Architect INTP

The Keirsey Temperament Sites   Assessment
www.temperament.net and keirsey.com

David Mark Keirsey, son of David West Keirsey (the designer of the Keirsey test) is listed as Webmaster for both sites, which essentially meet the same ends. They provide, free of charge, the Keirsey Temperament tests with analysis and they discuss the book, *Please Understand Me.*

Myers-Briggs Type Indicator (MBTI)

The MBTI was developed by Isabel Myers and Katharine Briggs as an application of Carl Jung's theory of personality types. By assessing how you perceive and judge information through thoughts or feelings, the MBTI identifies you as one of 16 possible types, made up of four preferences. The preferences are:

- **Extraverted or Introverted:** Extraverts draw energy from the people, events, and things in their environment; introverts draw energy from thoughts, feelings, and impressions of their inner world.

- **Sensing or iNtuitive:** We take in and absorb information either through using our senses (Sensing), or by relying on our instincts (iNtuitive).

- **Thinking or Feeling:** We make decisions either by thinking—deciding based on logic and objective consideration—or by feeling—using our personal, subjective value systems.

- **Judging or Perceiving.** Perception involves awareness of things, people, happenings, or ideas; judgment involves determining conclusions about perceptions.

Although your initial perception of this page may be a fear that you have entered a romance page, please look a little further. HumanMetrics includes a free, 72-question Myers-Briggs test, and uses www.keirsey.com and typelogic.com to explain your type. If you're not willing to pay $30-$50 for a more detailed Myers-Briggs test, this is an excellent place to start.

Other tests:

Designed to help students and youth make career and education plans, this site profiles people with interesting careers, reports labor market information, highlights innovative programs, and examines the career/life planning process. The interactive 10 Step Career Planning Guide is thorough and unique, and provides some incredible resources. It

helps you determine your top three work values; whether you are an introvert or extrovert; your three most dominant learning styles; your strongest transferable work skills; your top three interest categories; a sampling of your list of options; a career you have researched and three you plan to research; three people/organizations you can turn to for support; short- and long-term goals; and short- and long-term action plan goals and the steps needed to achieve them. The test is quite long, but worth the effort, and you can save your results and return to them at any time.

Platinum Rule
www.platinumrule.com

This site offers two great tests, the first of which, the Platinum Rule, will help you develop stronger business relationships and better interpersonal skills by typifying you as a director, relater, socializer, or thinker. By answering 18 questions concerning your work and social styles, you can understand your relations and compatibility with others, as well as determine others' personality styles and improve your productivity and career prospects. Completion of the test automatically adds you to a mailing list, through which you receive seven free, weekly articles on how to improve various facets of your personal and professional life. You can cancel the emailed articles at any time after receiving the first, but they're definitely interesting and worth your time.

The other test determines your charisma quotient, and provides interesting tips to improve the seven keys of personal charisma. The 21 questions lead you to ideas for improving your charisma by speaking with authority, presenting effective silent messages and images, listening attentively, increasing your persuasiveness, aptly using space and time, maximizing your adaptability, and expanding your vision and ideas. It also includes a newsletter, from which you may unsubscribe after the first email.

IQ Test
www.iqtest.com

This entertaining test provides your basic IQ assessment when you answer 38 questions. A complete assessment is available for $9.95, and includes information about "The Thirteen Abilities": Visual Apprehension, Spatial, Arithmetic, Logical, General Knowledge, Rote Utilization, Spelling, Intuition, Short Term Memory, Vocabulary, Geometric, Algebraic, and Computational Speed. This test claims to hit within 5 points of the professional tests. Those abilities in which you score far higher than your general IQ Score may indicate that you have special talents which could be useful in certain careers. Abilities in which you score lower than your general IQ Score may be areas you could improve with additional study and practice.

College Board Career Search	Assessment
www.collegeboard.org/careerhtml/searchQues.html	

This questionnaire asks you to identify your temperaments (how do you feel about…?), abilities (how good are you at…?), ideal working conditions (indoors or outdoors?), anticipated education level, interest areas, salary requirements, and employment outlook requirements. At the end of the test, up to 30 top careers are identified and you can read about the nature of work, working conditions, employment, training, job outlook, earnings, related occupations, and sources of additional information for each.

Kingdomality	Assessment
www.kingdomality.com	

By answering eight simple questions, you can determine what career you would have held in a medieval kingdom. The fun interface assigns you to careers like "the discoverer," "the benevolent ruler," "the dreamer minstrel," "the black knight,"

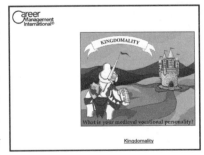

and many more. In addition to describing the tasks assigned to your career in medieval times, Kingdomality creates an excellent, easily understood association with current career roles for which your answers qualify.

If, after taking any of these tests, you are interested in finding out more general information about different jobs, the following sites offer a variety of information about different careers:

JobProfiles   Career Profiles
www.jobprofiles.com

This unique site lists the responses of successful businesspeople with careers in a variety of different areas, divided into agriculture and nature, arts and sports, business and communications, construction and manufacturing, education and science, government, health and social services, retail and wholesale, and other. The participants, selected from their memberships in associations, unions, and business organizations, filled out the same 15-question questionnaire, making the careers easy to compare. The questions assess the respondents' backgrounds, stresses and rewards associated with the different jobs, and future challenges and advice.

Occupational Outlook Handbook   Career Profiles
stats.bls.gov/ocohome.htm

The Bureau of Labor Statistics updates this guide on a semi-annual basis, providing one of the most thorough sources for career information. You may search by keywords for information on a specific career, in the following categories:

◆ Nature of Work

◆ Working Conditions

◆ Employment

◆ Training/Qualifications/Advancement

◆ Job Outlook

◆ Earnings

◆ Related Occupations

◆ Additional Information

Professional Organizations

Professional organizations, in which people participate based on their careers, industries, and a variety of other interests, envelop a wide spectrum of associations and membership organizations. Some of these organizations provide membership based on the individual's interests or career; others are based on the organization. Members can participate in networking activities, receive publications related to the career or industry, opt for special discounts on insurance and other programs, participate in award and recognition programs, study to achieve certifications for their field, and receive many additional benefits.

Joining these organizations either as a full member or an associate entitles you to these benefits, but many of these groups also provide excellent resources for people interested in careers or industries which they represent. You can easily learn the political involvement of the organizations represented, important news affecting the industry or careers, upcoming meetings (many of which non-members can attend at an increased fee)…and the list goes on.

I've included a few of the larger organizations, which offer a variety of useful information online. If you seek information about organizations for specific industries or career interests and the following list is not sufficient, refer to the search engine list in Chapter

1, through which you can focus a search on your targeted career or industry, as well as search for keywords that may help you narrow the organizations which meet your needs.

American Society of Association Executives   Organization
www.asaenet.org

With over 23,000 members worldwide, the American Society of Association Executives (ASAE) is the leading organization for association managers. Its membership is comprised of those who manage trade associations, individual membership societies, voluntary organizations, and other not-for-profit associations, as well as those who provide products and services to associations.

This site not only presents a wealth of information for anyone interested in working for an association; it also provides information about the organizations to which its members belong through directories of Associations Online, Association Management Companies, and U.S. and International Convention Centers and Convention Bureaus. These directories provide Web site links and contact information for the different organizations.

National Council of Nonprofit Associations   Organization
www.ncna.org

A network of 40 state and regional associations with a collective membership of more than 20,000 community nonprofits, the National Council of Nonprofit Associations (NCNA) serves as an excellent gateway into the nonprofit sector. Although the national organization may not provide the information you seek, it will direct you to the Web sites (or contact information) for its state and regional members.

These members can provide you with a myriad of information about nonprofits within their state, including contact information and Web site links, as well as jobs available within these nonprofits. The state and regional membership organizations also provide information about special projects in which they and their members are involved, information about the nonprofit sector as a whole, and much more.

Independent Sector **www.independentsector.org**	Organization

Independent Sector (IS), a national coalition of nonprofit organizations, includes foundations, nonprofits of all sizes, and Fortune 500 corporations with strong commitments to community involvement. The site provides excellent information about the nonprofit sector, including a basic definition of, statistics for, and pertinent news relating to the sector. You can also find a job on the site through a modest listing of members' employment opportunities.

Women Work! **www.womenwork.org**	Organization

Women Work! is dedicated to empowering women from diverse backgrounds and helping them achieve economic self-sufficiency. The organization works with local programs, federal, state and local government agencies, and other women's economic justice advocates to assure women's education and training programs re-

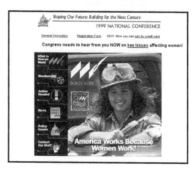

main on the cutting edge. It provides special projects, publications, and other resource materials that cover a wide range of service delivery and public policy issues critical to women's employment and training programs.

Women Work! is not purely for women with a lower economic standing; it also advocates for fair pay, better and more affordable child care and health care, pushes for increases to minimum wage, and provides counseling, education, and employment programs for women.

U.S. Chamber of Commerce   Organization
www.uschamber.org

The U.S. Chamber of Commerce represents nearly three million companies, 3,000 state and local chambers, 775 business associations and 85 American Chambers of Commerce abroad. It provides an extensive variety of information, from Congressional schedules and a list of relevant events, to information on nearly every policy or major issue that will affect business, to advocacy resources. This is an excellent site through which you can quickly determine some of the hot topics you might encounter in different organizations.

You can also browse through current position openings, descriptions of employee benefits, internship openings, and a variety of other information pertinent to working with the Chamber of Commerce.

Institute of Management Consultants	Organization
www.imcusa.org	

The Institute of Management Consultants (IMC) represents management consultants in the U.S. and overseas. IMC provides you with some excellent guidelines for professional behavior, including publicly acceptable means of verifying individual practitioners' qualifications and a Code of Ethics governing professional practice. Professional development opportunities include certification (Certified Management Consultant designation), conferences and workshops, and special interest groups. The organization also provides a helpful resource library and an online version of *The IMC Times,* which not only provides you with some interesting articles concerning consulting, but also offers valuable consulting resources.

Networking Resources

There are so many resources online that you can use to network your way into your dream job. Perhaps the most easily recognized are listservs and newsgroups, both of which use email to communicate between participants, and chat rooms, which enable users to conduct real-time conversations about the topics which interest them. In some cases, you can even "dump" your resume into a newsgroup or listserv. Be careful, because the result may provide more responses than you can handle! You may be swarmed by a variety of headhunters, direct marketers, and recruiters who have found the use of the word "Netscape" in your list of known computer applications. Positives and negatives exist for these online networking tools, but all three provide useful resources to the active job seeker.

Listservs

Perhaps the easiest and most rewarding networking resources, listservs are free and very passive, once you have subscribed to them for the first time. They're called listservs, and are also known as listserves, mailing lists, email lists, or list services. You can subscribe to most listservs simply by sending your name and email address to the list server. You are then automatically added to the virtual bcc (blind carbon copy) list and can read the conversations generated among the list participants.

Listservs provide a lively, interesting way to network online. Where else can you connect with hundreds of professionals with joint interests in a nearly instantaneous manner… in a forum where everyone can comfortably express their opinions and share their experiences? Not only can you gain valuable information about the working environment within a particular company from an individual within that company; you can also gain a better feel for the public's opinion of that company (customers, clients, contractors, etc.). Take that information well into account, but with a grain of salt, when you are considering your next career steps! On one hand, you may get some valuable advice that helps you in the career negotiation process; on the other, you may encounter a disgruntled employee who sours your opinion of a perfectly good company! You can also use listservs to gauge benefits and salary information from your peers.

Although they're invaluable, listservs do contain some minor pitfalls: users can digress from the main focus of the list, sometimes generating scores of bickering messages, and subscribers may be overwhelmed by the hundreds of email messages posted to the groups each week. The number of messages received may be lessened by using a "digest" subscription method, which provides either one or several messages per day, each of which contains information or copies of all messages posted to the list that day.

Listservs that are moderated (managed by a facilitator who attempts to keep messages on topic) may avoid the digressions and off-topic posts. Some listservs are private and can be accessed by invitation only. You may also encounter lists that are "announcement only" (also known as ezines), through which information is generated by one source and distributed to a broad list of subscribers. This type of listserv does not enable members to respond to the postings; they are simply vehicles for providing "read only" material.

The first step in joining a listserv is the hardest. You can choose from thousands of possible topics, and can focus on a narrow geographic region or join an international networking group. Each listserv may have slightly differing guidelines for signing up and participating, but all adhere to the simple rules of netiquette described in Chapter 1. Make sure you read and archive the basic guidelines provided when you sign up for the list, and please do not post marketing and self-promoting messages to the group! In most cases, this provides grounds for your immediate dismissal.

Following are some excellent directories and services for researching which listserv to join:

Liszt	Listserv Directory
www.liszt.com	

This dynamic, easy-to-use site provides over 90,095 mailing lists through which you can pick and choose! Liszt recently merged its resources with Topica, a free listserv hosting service. Users can search Liszt by keyword, or can browse through a variety of categories. Liszt also provides a "junk filtering" option, through which users can select

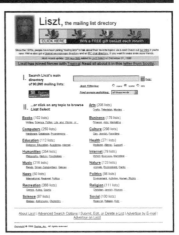

to filter irrelevant or private lists from their search, which can produce a maximum of 150 results per search.

Searching for the keyword "career" (with no filter) resulted in 73 mailing lists, from a career development book club to success tips and strategies for career planning success, to a career counselors list. A keyword search for "job" produced 108 lists, including jobs for artists and Christian ministry/business jobs.

eGroups	Listserv Directory
www.egroups.com	

eGroups also provides an easy, friendly format through which users can search for free listservs to which they may subscribe. However, eGroups takes the search process one step further and enables browsers to search more than 50 million messages, in addition to its 300,000 groups!

Every group within the eGroups network offers additional networking services (which may also be found with some other listservs not hosted by eGroups). These include an interactive group calendar through which members may notify each other or pertinent events; a "Group Document Vault," which securely stores files to be shared among the group; and a chat and talk area where users can talk online to group members (including free Internet voice telephone service, even for long distance and conference calls). eGroups is advertising-based, so users will see a small advertisement banner on each message distributed to the group; however, all lists enforce a heavy "anti-spam" policy, which filters out a considerable amount of junk mail.

Newsgroups

Other online resources include newsgroups, which function in similar ways to listservs by providing networking via email; however, users must actively select the newsgroups in which they are interested each time they seek to access the messages. Newsgroups are rarely moderated, which makes them more susceptible to spam, junk, and irritating pranksters. Information seekers will also encounter an overwhelming number of messages posted to these lists, so please practice some caution in believing everything you read! These sources can provide a variety of interesting and useful information, and should not be discounted based on the freedom of speech that is actively practiced herein.

Your access to newsgroups is determined by your ISP, which subscribes to a selected group of listservs. Don't worry about the resources being too few; many ISPs provide access to so many groups that you can easily be overwhelmed! To start using newsgroups, you'll experience the least confusion by asking your ISP for instructions about connecting to their newsgroup server. Once you have connected to your ISP's service, you can search through a wide assortment of useful and irreverant groups...the key is to keep an open mind while you search for the end result.

If you are frustrated with newsgroups, several sites provide concise, easy-to-understand directions, as well as lists of newsgroups to which you may wish to subscribe:

◆ www.xs4all.nl/~wijnands/nnq/grouplists.html

◆ www.dejanews.com

◆ www.liszt.com/news

Online Chat/Internet Relay Chat

Although extremely effective networking tools, chat rooms have caused a variety of troubles for novices to cyberspace. Also known as Internet Relay Chat (IRC), chat provides ways for users to communicate, one-on-one or in groups, by typing messages which are instantly viewed by others on their computer screens.

America Online has provided a variety of chat areas for its sub-scribers for many years, and offers free, interactive services called Instant Messenger and ICQ, through which AOL members and non-members may chat. You can easily search on these services for people with similar interests and join moderated or un-moderated chat sessions. Some resume posting sites covered in Chapter 4 offer their own, private chat areas for members. These and other services enable you to gain instant answers to your career questions.

Protect Your Most Valuable Asset...Yourself!

Although these networking tools can be useful in your job search, they also carry their share of problems. Be careful to whom you provide personal information. You wouldn't give your phone number and address to a stranger in a bar or to someone who started following you home one night, would you? Do you provide your credit card number to every telemarketer who calls? Be smart about using on-line resources; protect yourself and your job search. If you get into trouble, the following resources can help you out:

- Women Halting Online Abuse—www.haltabuse.org—educates about online harassment, empowers victims of harassment, and formulates voluntary policies that systems can adopt in order to create harassment-free environments.

- Coalition Against Unsolicited Commercial Email—www.cauce.org—provides information about the problems of junk email, some proposed solutions, and resources for Internet users to make informed choices about the issues surrounding junk email.

- CyberAngels—www.cyberangels.org—educates Internet users about online safety, privacy, and how to get the most out of the Internet.

3

CREATE GREAT RESUMES AND COVER LETTERS

Nearly every job search contains three major components: resume, cover letter, and interview. In order to successfully survive the job search process, you need to hone your skills in each of these areas. Fortunately, a variety of online and offline resources exist to help you really "wow" potential employers.

First, however, you need to familiarize yourself with the basics of these tools... and the basics have changed. In addition to providing some starting tips and advice about resumes and cover letters, this chapter will also teach you some special ways in which the Internet has forever changed the dynamics of these job search tools. Chapter 6 focuses on the steps that follow later in the job search process: interviews and salary negotiations.

Building the Perfect Resume

The resume continues to be one of the most important written documents you will use in your job search. Not only does an excellent resume clearly communicate your qualifications to potential employers, it also focuses on what they need and how you can provide solutions for them. Show how your experience can help them prepare for a successful future.

Before venturing into the dynamics of electronic resumes, take some time to update your traditional, paper resume. It will serve as the basis from which you develop other resumes, and **you always need to provide a classic, well-organized, nicely designed paper resume during an interview.** Several books provide more in-depth coverage of resume development, and can be located through www.impactpublications.com, your local library, or a bookstore:

- *Dynamite Resumes*, by Ron and Caryl Krannich
- *The Savvy Resume Writer*, by Ron and Caryl Krannich
- *Resume Winners from the Pros*, by Wendy Enelow
- *Resumes for Dummies*, by Joyce Lain Kennedy
- *Haldane's Best Resumes for Professionals*, by Bernard Haldane Associates

Several online sites focus specifically on resumes tips and tricks. Those sites, when used with the information included in this chapter, will help you produce a high quality, well-written resume:

Resumania	Resume Writing
www.resumania.com	

This entertaining site provides a lighter look at the world of resume writing. It provides examples of blunders and mishaps from real-life resumes. This site should help you improve your resume writing skills and avoid making careless errors.

The site also provides an excerpt from *Job Hunting for Dummies*: "The 12 Cardinal Sins of Resume Writing," which include unprofessionalism, carelessness, cuteness and cleverness, irrelevance and fluff, vagueness or jargon, misrepresentation, over-kill, underwhelming, longwindedness, editorializing, overpersonalizing, and resumespeak. Take a moment to browse through the examples and learn how to avoid making a fool of yourself and your resume.

4resumes   Resumes
www.4resumes.com

Filled with an excellent assortment of links to helpful hints and interactive resources, this site will prove extremely helpful toward your resume and cover letter preparation. In addition to listing some of the major resume boards and cover letter and resume writing tips, 4resumes provides links to certified career coaches and reputable guides.

4Resumes includes a section on resume lies, including survey information that states "more than half of all employers have discovered outright lies while verifying information on job applications." There's also advice on how to squeeze every advantage from your qualifications, tell the truth, and still get your resume noticed.

ProvenResumes.com   Resume Writing
www.provenresumes.com

It's hard to find more thorough resume advice online—this site really covers all of the bases. Created by the author of the *Proven Resumes* series, this site claims to provide "resume strategies that have doubled interview rates and landed 10% to 50% higher salaries!" The site also features information about career specific resume tips, including those geared to college students, nonprofits, teachers, military, and management.

Users follow a free, simple and interesting workshop format, including before and after examples, design and content, popular resume styles, how to identify and market skills, solutions to employers' needs, and confidence building strategies. You can also gain some general information about email and scannable resumes.

The most important part of building a resume is to keep focused on your purpose. A resume creates the opportunity for you to clearly demonstrate to potential employers how your past performance will affect their future. Present clear, concise examples that prove you are the candidate who will fulfill the responsibilities of the job for which they are hiring. In the books listed above, as well as a variety of other sources, you will encounter three major types of resumes, although the combination resume is most effective:

- **Chronological resumes** (sometimes referred to as obituary resumes) outline employment history according to dates of employment, and show your responsibilities and titles for each job. These resumes function most effectively for job seekers with a progressive record of work experience, who seek to advance within an occupational field.

- **Functional resumes** show patterns of skills and accomplishments instead of focusing on titles, employers, and employment dates. These resumes will most appropriately help those making a significant career change, entering the work world for the first time, or re-entering the work world after a long absence. They also can be useful if your work experience does not clearly support your objective.

- **Combination resumes** combine the best of chronological and functional resumes by stressing patterns of accomplishments and skills as well as work history. If you wish to change to a job in a related career field, this resume provides the best choice for you.

Whatever the format, every resume should show that you are a purposeful job seeker who has established realistic career goals that you would like to achieve. Employers should also gain the feeling that you will provide them with a productive, responsible worker who will strongly benefit their organization.

Primary Categories for Effective Resumes

Although resumes will vary from candidate to candidate, based on personal style and the job for which you are applying, there are several standard categories that are familiar to any resume:

- ◆ **Contact information:** Your name, address, phone, and email. If you don't have a personal email address, get one. Several helpful online services, such as www.hotmail.com, www.ivillage.com, and many others, will provide you with an email account, free of charge, which you can check via any Web browser. Avoid using your work email, unless you plan on your employer learning about your job search.

- ◆ **Objective:** Should be relevant to your skills, employers' needs, and the information on your resume. An objective sets the organization of your resume, showing that you have purpose and have determined specific job and career goals to fulfill. Without an objective, employers must guess about your career future, and may be unclear whether you are on track with their company's needs. By creating a firm base for your resume, you control the manner in which your qualifications and capabilities are interpreted. Show em-

Combination   **MELISSA C. ADAMS**

14 Third Avenue   Springfield, OH 45504   MCAdams@olt.com   222/555-1212

OBJECTIVE:	To create and manage an interactive Web site that excels in the Internet marketplace.

AREAS OF EFFECTIVENESS

ADMINISTRATION:	Supervised creation and development of Web page and marketing programs. Coordinated media relations, desktop publishing, and advertising for online and print publications.
COMMUNICATION:	Trained staff on software applications and Internet communications. Experienced writer of e-zine, media releases, and promotional materials. Created and edited brochures, pamphlets, and booklets.
PLANNING:	Planned and created 65 page Web site. Developed new procedures for Web maintenance. Determined best procedures for securing print and electronic advertising, Web hosting, and software and hardware purchase.
WORK HISTORY:	Director of Electronic Relations, Synergy Dynamics, 1997 to present.
	Manager and Director of Communications and Information Services, American Association of Nonprofits, 1995-1997.
	Systems Analyst and Webmaster, Department of Education, Matrix Technologies, inc., 1994-1995.
EDUCATION:	M.A. in Communications Management. Ohio State University, Columbus, OH, 1994.
	B.A. in English, Virginia Tech University, Blacksburg, VA, 1991.

SUPPLEMENTAL INFORMATION

Technical Highlights
Microsoft Office, WordPerfect, Pagemaker, Photoshop, GoLive, Netscape, Listserv administration, Web site development tools, PC operating systems, UNIX, and other systems, languages, and programs.

Professional Affiliations
Female Tech Directors Association, SafeNET, Ohio Web Designers Network.

ployers that you truly know what you would like to do; you are, after all, seeking a job that will fit your career future.

◆ **Experience/Work History:** Employers' names, employment dates, position held, responsibilities, achievements/contributions, and special skills/abilities. This is your place to shine, to show how the patterns of the past will benefit an employer's future. This area clearly communicates your strengths to employers by presenting your major accomplishments. Use numbers and percentages to demonstrate realized achievements. Highlight your special awards and recognition so prospective employers will realize how you stand out from the crowd.

◆ **Educational background:** Degree, graduation date, institution, and special highlights/achievements. Special training courses can also be included in this category, if related to your objective and skills.

You can also create some specialized areas on your resume—just make sure they relate to your objective, work history, and skills background:

◆ Military experience

◆ Community involvement, including volunteer activities and political offices held, if relevant

◆ Professional affiliations

◆ Special skills

◆ Related interests and activities

◆ Personal statement

Resume Death Sentences

Employers don't like to waste their time or company's resources, so they will be on the lookout for resumes that can be quickly removed from consideration. Give your resume a fighting chance, not a quick trip to the trash can, by following a few simple guidelines:

- **Do not include salary expectations or references on your resume.** Demonstrate your value to employers and determine the worth of the position before you discuss salary. Spend some time researching what other professionals in similar positions and geographic locations receive in compensation, as discussed in Chapter 6. Benefits play such a big part in compensation discussions that you will want some idea of what the employer offers in this area, as well.

- **Guard your references with the same philosophy.** Your references are doing you a favor by offering information about the many benefits they witnessed you provide to prior employers, and how well you would apply work experiences in a new job. Prepare them for reference calls so that they may most effectively help you. Let them know to which employers you have provided their contact information, and brief descriptions of the jobs for which you have applied. Good references will think in advance about their knowledge of your abilities and how you would be the BEST fit an employer could gain for this job.

- **Don't add irrelevant personal information,** such as your weight, height, age, or spouse's name. These attributes will not affect your ability to handle the job, and will cause the employer to wonder whether or not you will be able to successfully function in a workplace with so many concerns!

◆ **Don't leave unexplained time gaps.** Your resume must speak for itself, since you will not be in the room when an employer first reviews it. Did you take time off to attend school full-time or did you tour Germany to increase your language skills and cultural perspective? Work it into your resume so you don't leave the employer with unanswered questions, such as whether you ran afoul of the law, or did you lose complete focus of your career for that unexplained time period?

◆ You can never proofread your resume enough. Make it error-free or don't send it! Some common mistakes good proofreading will avoid: misspellings, bad grammar, wordiness, and poor punctuation.

◆ Steer clear of too much self-praise. Stick to the facts to create a more effective impact.

◆ Avoid using the word "I" in your resume.

How the Internet Has Changed Resumes

The Internet has added some important advantages to the resume process. Both job seekers and employers experience a quicker turnaround between the time a job is announced and the time in which candidates submit resumes. Job seekers no longer need worry about expensive career counseling and printing costs (the Internet enables them to narrow down the number of hard copy resumes they will print). Employers can post jobs to their own Web sites at no cost; they can also bypass expensive recruiters and use Internet sites such as Monster.com and Headhunter.net to increase their cost savings. Both groups experience an extended presence in the job marketplace, not only in the length of time a job or resume remains "active" and visible, but also in its global reach. Now, the administrative job originally listed in your local paper may be seen by someone halfway across the world, and he or she may be the most eligible candidate for the job. Your competition has increased on a significant level.

Less is no longer more. Providing more information now increases your chances of being found online, so you need to learn how to increase its effectiveness without adding unnecessary clutter. Action verbs are "out," and power keywords are the "hot" trend for effective resumes. Browse through some of the online resumes to familiarize yourself with some of the effects that work best, but be prepared to also find some examples of how NOT to write a resume. You'll quickly learn that some elements of traditional resumes, such as full sentences, are not necessarily the best elements to use. You can also look into the following books for excellent advice about preparing an online resume:

- *Internet Resumes*, by Pete Weddle
- *Electronic Resumes & Online Networking*, by Rebecca Smith
- *Cyberspace Resume Kit*, by Mary B. Nemnich and Fred Jandt

Many resume posting services now offer the opportunity for job seekers to post an anonymous or "confidential" resume, in order to protect their current job status. Prospective employers see all of the information intended to be seen, but when they are ready to contact the candidate, the resume service serves as the intermediary between job seeker and employer. If you are still concerned about your present employer learning that you are seeking a job, you may also want to "camouflage" your resume so that your present and past employers are not listed by name or location. Depending on the type of jobs you have held, you may need to work even harder to hide your identity, by "disguising" some of the activities you have completed in your work. This should not be considered dishonest (unless, of course, you are providing inaccurate information about your past experience!); with the ease of accessibility provided by the Internet, most employers will understand your need for confidentiality.

Many sites can automatically contact the candidate to advise them that a specific employer has requested contact information about them, and the candidate decides whether or not to they wish to be contacted by the employer. Other sites will forward the employer's query directly to the job seeker via an alias, again leaving the matter in the job seeker's hands. Out of common courtesy, do respond to these services; otherwise, the employer may be left wondering whether the automated service really forwarded their request to you.

Email Resumes

If you locate an interesting job opportunity online, you may need to send an email resume, but be careful when using this tool! Most employers prefer NOT to receive unsolicited, emailed resumes, so do not email your resume unless specifically requested to. Why? Computer viruses. They "infect" every computer upon which they are run, and can interfere with the proper operations of the computer and the programs it runs. Imagine your embarrassment, and the immediate removal of your resume from consideration, if you send a virus to a potential employer!

Essentially, the safest way to make sure that you will not embarrass yourself by sending a virus in ANY communications addressed to a potential employer: install virus-protection software on your computer, and check a reputable source for information on how to remove viruses from your computer. Some of the top virus information and protection resources include:

◆ www.mcafee.com

◆ www.symantec.com

If an employer requests an email resume and you have prepared your computer to not pass on viruses, you need to prepare your resume to deliver optimal impact. If you have followed the hints listed above concerning traditional resume preparation, you are ready to take that ideal resume, tear it apart, and reformat it for email.

High-Powered Key Words for Electronic Resumes

accomplish	counsel	facilitate	investigate
achievement	create	file	launch
advise	decrease	fix	learn
advocate	delegate	focus	lecture
analyze	demonstrate	found	maintain
appoint	design	fund	manage
arrange	detail	generate	monitor
assemble	determine	guide	motivate
assign	develop	hire	negotiate
assist	direct	identify	organize
attend	discover	implement	plan
audit	edit	improve	prepare
calculate	educate	increase	prevent
collaborate	eliminate	influence	produce
communicate	enable	inform	project
complete	enforce	innovate	promote
computer	ensure	install	publish
conceptualize	equip	instruct	recruit
conduct	establish	integrate	solve
consult	exceed	interpret	streamline
contribute	expand	introduce	supervise
coordinate	expedite	invent	train

Save your resume as a text file with no formatting or as an ascii text file. Close and reopen it to remove special formatting such as bolding, columns, graphical lines, etcetera. You should also delete all of the bullets and replace them either with asterisks or single dashes. Clean up large spaces left by conversion of tabs to simple text format.

At the top, enter your name, address, phone number, and email address and make sure they are left justified. All text (headers as well as descriptive paragraphs!) should be flush left with a ragged right margin. Avoid adding too many hard returns between paragraphs; they either will not work the way you intend them or they will look awkward, as if you are attempting to make the resume as long as possible.

To check the formatting of the resume, either cut and paste it (preferred) into the body of or attach it to an email message addressed to yourself. Remember to remove the following elements, because you can never be sure how they will appear in your resume's final electronic version:

- bullets
- tabs
- boxes
- hyphenated line breaks
- special symbols, other than those you see pictured on your keyboard
- centering
- bold
- italics

Do not forget about your keywords! Some people even include a special keywords section on their resume. On page 48 are possible

Electronic

MELISSA C. ADAMS
14 Third Avenue, Springfield, OH 45504
MCAdams@olt.com * 222/555-1212

OBJECTIVE:
To create and manage an interactive Web site that
excels in the Internet marketplace.

AREAS OF EFFECTIVENESS

ADMINISTRATION:
Supervised creation and development of Web page and
marketing programs. Coordinated media relations,
desktop publishing, and advertising for online and
print publications.

COMMUNICATION:
Trained staff on software applications and Internet
communications. Experienced writer of e-zine, media
releases, and promotional materials. Created and
edited brochures, pamphlets, and booklets.

PLANNING:
Planned and created 65 page Web site. Developed new
procedures for Web maintenance. Determined best
procedures for securing print and electronic
advertising, Web hosting, and software and hardware
purchase.

WORK HISTORY:
Director of Electronic Relations, Synergy Dynamics,
1997 to present.

Director of Communications and Information Services,
American Association of Nonprofits, 1996-1997.

Manager Communications and Information Services,
American Association of Nonprofits, 1995-1996.

Systems Analyst and Webmaster, Department of
Education, Matrix Technologies, inc., 1994-1995.

Information Technology Assistant, University
Relations, Ohio State University, 1994.

International Assistant, National Librarians'
Council, 1992-1994.

Training Secretary, National Librarians' Council,
1991-1992.

EDUCATION:
M.A. in Communications Management. Ohio State
University, Columbus, OH, 1994.

B.A. in English, Virginia Tech University,
Blacksburg, VA, 1991.

SUPPLEMENTAL INFORMATION

Computer Skills Highlights:

Microsoft Office, WordPerfect, Pagemaker, Photoshop,
GoLive, Netscape, Listserv administration, Web site
development tools, PC operating systems, UNIX, and
other systems, languages, and programs.

Professional Affiliations:

Female Tech Directors Association, SafeNET, Ohio Web
Designers Network.

Language Skills:

German, Spanish.

Volunteer Work:

Appointed newsletter editor and Web site designer,
Gamma Omega Central Ohio Alumnae Chapter.

Keyword Summary:

achievement, advisor, analyze, assist, communicate,
computer, conceptualization, conduct, consult,
contributor, delegate, designer, developer, editor,
exceed, generate, guide, identify, improve, increase,
innovative, launch, manage, motivate, negotiator,
project, publish, recruit, streamline, and supervise.

References and samples available upon request.

keywords for which employers might search; whenever possible, use a noun form of these words. Career-specific keywords can be found in ads and job postings. List the qualifications, technical expertise, industry jargon, product knowledge, and personality traits that employers are seeking within your field. Or, try looking through search engines to see what "hot terminology" people are using!

Scannable Resumes

If you need to submit a scannable resume, be prepared. Basically, a scanner searches for keywords that will match the company's needs. With a few minor adjustments, you can adapt your Internet resume to fit the scannable format:

- ◆ Your name should be on top of all pages
- ◆ Use 10-14 point, San serif font—san means without the serifs (the small stroke at the ends of letter—**Times** and **Garamond** are serifs, **Univers** and **Arial** are san serifs.)
- ◆ No italics, graphics, or underlines; boldface may be okay
- ◆ Avoid using horizontal or vertical lines
- ◆ Laser printers provide the clearest results; send originals
- ◆ Beware of abbreviations; many scanning programs will read these as spelling errors
- ◆ Avoid columns
- ◆ Use one-sided, light-colored paper
- ◆ Do not use staples

HTML Resumes

So, you want to look like a real pro, eh? Make sure you are a real pro before attempting to create an HTML resume, and keep in mind that no matter how well you or a friend you hire design Web pages, there are some problems that you will probably run into. In order to impress a potential employer during my last job search (they were seeking someone with Web design experience), I created an HTML resume. During the interview, my resume was produced, and we discussed the final format. Much to my dismay, the interviewer had viewed the resume while using a larger font size for his screen, which translated to a larger font for the printer, and resulted in a completely different layout than I had initially designed. The large type really destroyed my carefully spaced categories! In the end, my paper copy resume saved my day, but I really had to think quickly to explain the awkward formatting of the Web resume.

Try to follow the same formatting guidelines as for regular resumes. Yes, you want to demonstrate your Web design prowess, but unless you are seeking a job as a complex Web designer, you may end up confusing your end result with having fun. You should provide a resume that is easily navigated, that highlights your accomplishments, and that clearly demonstrates to potential employers what you will contribute to their organization.

It's up to you whether to include a picture of yourself, but it's safest to avoid doing so. At least fifty percent of employers will dislike some aspect of your photo, and you. The photo provides an employer with things to pick apart—your hairstyle, eyes, color, smile, or dress. Why provide them with that opportunity? Stick with the standards and play it safe.

Links to different pages cause problems because the recruiter will not spend the time clicking onto all of these sub-pages, printing them out, and providing them to personnel!

Killer Cover Letters

In order to pull together the killer job application package, you need to precede your resume with a cover letter that clearly defines how your skills and experience will meet and exceed the employer's needs. Despite the rapid move toward online job searching, some of the standard rules have remained the same. One of the easiest ways to provide this information is to constantly consider ways in which your background matches the job description, and to figure out how it surpasses those skills. Employers need employees who can "think outside the box" and provide the most value for their money.

Some reliable books to consult for effective cover letter creation include:

- *Cover Letters That Knock 'Em Dead*, by Martin Yate
- *Haldane's Best Cover Letters for Professionals*, by Bernard Haldane Associates
- *Dynamite Cover Letters*, by Ron and Caryl Krannich

The same basic writing rules apply to cover letters as to resumes:

- You can never check your cover letter enough times for typographical and grammatical errors
- Avoid wordiness or unclear thoughts
- Use keywords
- Include adequate and correct contact information
- Avoid using the elements defined on page 49

Important Cover Letter Elements

Cover letters, however, also require additional "do's and don'ts," beyond your resume. Above all else, make sure your cover letter is tailored and targeted toward the specific job. You are also trying to communicate your value to the employer, based on your skills and accomplishments, and what patterns of performance you will bring to the job. As simple as it may sound, you want to convince the employer that this job also meets your needs—instilling confidence that the match would be as good for you as for the employer. Keep your sentences and paragraphs short, concise, and focused. Fill your cover letter with key words that are easily scannable, reinforced with statistics and examples.

Four basic elements will help you convey these impressions, as well as show that you can compose business communications with style and accuracy:

Address/Contact Information

Perhaps one of the most important, yet frequently bypassed or incorrectly included, steps to writing a cover letter is the inclusion of the proper contact's name and title. Take an extra few minutes to search the company's online employee directory, or call and ask for the name and title of the director for the department for which the position is listed (example: if the job title was public relations assistant, ask for the name of the director of public relations.). If you cannot determine a personal contact, address the letter to a gender-neutral title, such as "Dear Employer." "To Whom It May Concern" usually implies that you didn't attempt to do simple homework.

Lead-in Paragraph

Another important element to your cover letter is your lead-in paragraph. You should start with a snappy, interesting lead in which you clearly identify the job for which you are applying. Be confident that you are the best candidate for the job, and express your confidence (but not cockiness!) through strong statements to that effect. Be direct and to the point, so the letter recipient immediately recognizes the purpose of your letter.

Middle Paragraph(s)

This is your chance to clearly demonstrate how the skills and experience listed in your resume meet and exceed the expectations listed in the job description. You can also show how your career objective(s) will be satisfied by the available position. Since most readers spend no more than 20 to 30 seconds scanning the letter for key thoughts and words, make sure that you keep your content interesting, energetic, and active, while maintaining a personal, professional tone.

Final Paragraph

The final paragraph is equally as important. Rather than closing with a bland, run of the mill "I hope to hear from you," show that you are a proactive job seeker. An excellent closing that will impress many employers... "I look forward to meeting you... I will call on <date> to schedule an interview at your convenience." The most important requirement to this final paragraph is that you follow-up as you have indicated. Failing to do so indicates that you are not reliable and may drop the ball on the job.

How the Internet Has Changed Cover Letters

Following the basic information listed in the resume section will also prepare your cover letter for the Internet, but there are a few additional guidelines of which you should be aware. First, if an employer has indicated that attachments are acceptable, limit the number of attachments by combining your cover letter and resume into a single file. Use an attention-grabbing subject line, and include complete contact information at the end of your email message.

Even if you have included your cover letter in your resume attachment, you should also cut and paste it into the body of your email message. By including it in both places, you have ensured that the recipient will "meet" you through your email message, encouraging her to open your resume. You have also improved the chances that a scanner will catch words in your cover letter that may not be included in your resume, and that your cover letter will be printed at the same time as your resume. This helps ensure that anyone to whom your resume is passed will also receive a copy of your cover letter. Otherwise, the letter may become detached from the resume.

Top 10 Ways to Kill Your Electronic Cover Letter

1. Don't check for typos or misspellings.
2. Send the letter as a separate file attachment without first checking with the employer.
3. Don't include your contact information.
4. Skimp in your cover letter/email, stating only "Here's my application for your available position."
5. Don't include anything on your cover letter that isn't also on your resume.
6. Write a self-centered cover letter, with frequent use of "I," "me," and "my."
7. Include your salary requirements and/or references.
8. Address the letter "to whom it may concern."
9. Create an obvious form letter that's not tailored toward the specific job.
10. Write an amateurish, unprofessional letter.

MELISSA C. ADAMS
14 Third Avenue
Springfield, OH 45504

Mr. X. Y. Zeta
Vice President of Communications
Data Innovations Corporation
14 Hyatt Avenue
Springfield, OH   45504

Dear Mr. Zeta:

With my strong background in Web site design and
management, I bring the skills you need to fulfill
your Web site manager position (#36533) listed on
Monster.com. As a strong team leader who exhibits
achievements at every level, I would lead your staff
into the creation of a dynamic, highly-effective Web
network.

With nearly fifteen years of online experience, I
have consistently demonstrated my abilities to excel
on the Internet. In my current Web management
position, I designed, programmed, and promoted a top
travel Web site. In six months, traffic increased
from 150 to 1,000 hits per week, and income from the
online bookstore quadrupled in the first quarter and
has continued to grow.

Your expectations for this position would be quickly
met and exceeded through the application of my
background and skills. I will contact you next
Wednesday to answer any questions you may have about
my qualifications. Thank you for your time and
consideration.

Sincerely,

Melissa C. Adams
MCAdams@olt.com
222/555-1212

Many of the resume posting/job searching sites included in Chapter 4 contain special tips and tricks for successful resume and cover letter writing. However, specialized sites listed on pages 38-40 and 59-60 will help you prepare before diving into the resume posting/job searching sites. Many of these sites explore more than just resume and cover letter writing, so make sure you explore them to their fullest potential!

Knock 'Em Dead
www.knockemdead.com
Resumes, Cover Letters, & Interviews

Prepared by the author of the Knock 'Em Dead career series, this valuable site helps you prepare a resume and cover letter. The resume section starts out with a preparatory resume questionnaire and a proofreading checklist, as well as examples, templates, and tips for chronological, functional, and combination resumes. The cover letter section includes not only a questionnaire and checklist, but also samples: response to advertisements, broadcast cover letters, executive briefing style, and general cover letters. Users will also find helpful tips on interviews.

JobStar California
www.jobstar.org
Resumes and Cover Letters

Don't let the name fool you. Despite being tailored to job seekers in California, this site provides a wide variety of resources valuable to anyone searching for a new job! The resume section includes sample resumes, information about different resume styles (chronological, functional, electronic,

and curriculum vitae!), and information about electronic re-sume banks. Additionally, selected resume resources on the Web contain links to assistance for general job seekers, first-time job seekers, recent graduates, and technical job titles.

Don't miss the other helpful areas, especially the cover let-ter sections, which are hidden under the resume section. The career guides section features online career tests, guides for spe-cific careers, career guides in libraries, and books and software.

4

ONLINE RESUME POSTING AND JOB LISTING SITES

Now that you've learned the basics about the Internet, conducting online searches, and preparing your resume for potential employers, it's time to find those employers! Online resume posting and job listing sites provide two very distinct options, the first of which is a more passive process; the second requires real dynamism in your job search!

Most sites listed in this chapter include both resume posting and job listing features. Most of the sites do not specialize in one career field or geographic location; there are some exceptional sites, however, that will provide you with invaluable resources, no matter where you are or what you do.

Online Resume Posting Sites: The Basics

The familiar phrase "you get what you pay for" does NOT apply here! Unless the resume posting site represents a truly unique, obscure specialty, guarantees a job placement, or instantly makes you a millionaire, you're probably paying too much for resume posting sites that are not free to job seekers. As with traditional recruiting services, employers pay a premium for the resumes they preview, as well as additional fees if they hire a candidate.

The sites listed within this chapter contain three main methods for posting your resume: form resume, resume upload, or combination. Some may offer privacy or anonymity. If you want to ensure your current employer will not accidentally stumble across your resume online, check this out before you post!

- ◆ **Form resume databases**: job seekers fill out a form about their backgrounds and interests. They may select from a group of keywords which identify their talents. Usually includes contact information.

- ◆ **Resume upload databases**: job seekers upload or cut and paste their resumes to the database. No forms are filled out.

- ◆ **Combination upload/form resume databases**: job seekers fill out some basic contact information about themselves, and some other qualifying information (compensation, education level, full- or part-time, location) and upload their resume and possibly cover letter.

Before posting to an online resume bank, be prepared to encounter some possible frustrations, such as offers that don't match your resume or objectives or no response at all. Many of the online databases are overpopulated and your resume may not get noticed or may be misclassified unless you are using the proper keywords. You can try some of the specialized resume databases, but there's a chance you might miss some of the big recruiters. Have faith, and make sure your resume states clearly and succinctly what you seek.

Offers that are clearly not related to your background or interests can be turned into your advantage, so don't immediately dismiss them as a waste of your time. You never know when other opportunities might arise from the same recruiter. If you are approached for a position that does not match your objective, but matches some past job experience, respond that although you have worked in that capacity, your interests have changed. Does the recruiter know of any opportunities for someone with your objective? Your candor and professionalism may win you a useful ally who can help you find your dream job. Don't write off recruiters just because they are so busy that they made a mistake; their business probably means they work with a variety of companies who might be interested in you!

If your resume posting results in large amounts of junk mail, refrain from sending nasty emails to the offending emailer. Most likely, the message will just get bounced back to you. Worse yet, some of the responses you send will show that you have an active email account, and your email address may be distributed to many other junk email lists! If you notice persistent messages from a specific junk emailer, notify your ISP or check into email filtering programs.

Online Job Listing Sites: The Basics

In some ways, job listing sites may seem easier to use than the resume listing sites. Generally, you search the sites by keyword, company, or geographic location. However, you can easily end up spending a great deal of time looking through the many job listings posted on these sites. The more sophisticated, resume/job listing sites will forward your resume to employers you select with just one click.

How do you start searching? The sites vary dramatically in the way they are arranged, but here are a few tips that may make your search easier. First, think of your resume, especially the objective and your positive past job responsibilities. What did you enjoy doing, and what job aspects would you like to examine more fully? Look at your responses to the career assessment tests you took. Make a keyword list from the results of these processes, and enter some of these keywords into the job listing search engines. In many cases, using too many of these keywords might result in too narrow a search, with no results. If this happens, try a combination of one or two at a time. Identify your geographic area, and start searching!

4work

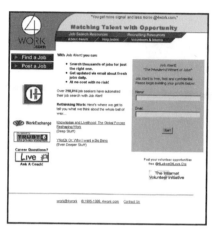

4work helps job seekers find jobs for free and employers and recruiters find and hire qualified people at a reasonable price. Not only for full- and part-time jobs, but also internships and volunteer activities. Job Alert! helps job seekers build profiles describing interests, abilities, and geographic preferences to receive email notification when opportunities fit their needs.

Standard Features:

Cost to see jobs: Free; registration required

Automatic job updates: Yes

Number of jobs: N/A

Specialty/Industry: All

Cost to post resume: Not Available

Posting period: N/A

Geographic coverage: International

Full- or part-time/contract: All

Special Features:

◆ Sponsors www.4LaborsofLove.org, The Internet Volunteer Initiative, the largest volunteer database on the Internet.

◆ Special interest topics include: associations, higher education, training, conferences and workshops, employment security, publications, other recruiting Web sites, relocation, resume services, temporary services.

◆ Very strong privacy measures.

www.4work.com

America's Job Bank

America's Job Bank enables job seekers to post resumes, create cover letters, track job searches, and develop a personal online career account. It is a partnership between the US Department of Labor and the state operated public Employment Service, which provides a labor exchange service to employers and job seekers through a network of 1800 offices throughout the United States.

Standard Features:

Cost to see jobs: Free; registration required

Automatic job updates: Yes

Number of jobs: Over 1,423,556

Specialty/Industry: All

Cost to post resume: Free; registration required

Posting period: 60 days

Geographic coverage: National

Full- or part-time/contract: All

Special Features:

◆ Comprehensive information on occupational outlook, including: general outlook, wages and trends, employers, state profile, resource library, and career exploration.

◆ America's Learning eXchange lets job seekers search for classroom courses, distance learning opportunities, Web- and computer-based training, educational programs, conference workshops, and seminars and for providers that offer them.

www.ajb.dni.us

Best Jobs USA

Best Jobs U.S.A. provides a variety of information on career fairs and employment events throughout the country. It lists corporate profiles and a variety of links to employment sites. Also includes the electronic version of *Employment Review*, a monthly publication filled with salary surveys, market trends, information on mergers, acquisitions, and layoffs, and contemporary workplace issues.

Standard Features:

Cost to see jobs: Free; registration required

Automatic job updates: Yes

Number of jobs: 16,000

Specialty/Industry: All

Cost to post resume: Free; registration required

Posting period: 1 year

Geographic coverage: International

Full- or part-time/contract: All

Special Features:

◆ Free Career Strength Report helps job seekers learn how potential employers perceive them and better understand the type of company for which they are best suited.

◆ Great listing of a variety of newsgroups available to job seekers, grouped by industry and geographic location.

◆ Free weekly e-zine provides job seekers with news, information, and tips to master today's workplace.

www.bestjobsusa.com

BrilliantPeople.com

BrilliantPeople.com provides job seekers with a more personalized touch... a network of more than 5,000 professional, industry-specific recruiters from over 900 offices in 35 countries. Users can search for jobs by keyword or through a specialized search form. A wide variety of career tools, including a weekly email newsletter, help job seekers improve their search abilities and success.

Standard Features:

Cost to see jobs: Free; registration required

Automatic job updates: Yes

Number of jobs: N/A

Specialty/Industry: All

Cost to post resume: Free; registration required

Posting period: N/A

Geographic coverage: International

Full- or part-time/contract: All

Special Features:

- ◆ "Ask a recruiter" enables job seekers to directly interact with recruiters to find out how job seekers can use recruiters to help them find a job.

- ◆ Career resources include: Career Planning, "Resumes: The Write Way to Present Yourself," Interviewing Techniques, Relocation, National Hiring Trends, and Industry Hiring Trends.

www.brilliantpeople.com

Career Dot Com

Career Dot Com, "the world's first recruitment site," was established in 1993, and has grown in leaps and bounds! Jobs are searchable through a variety of means, including Company, Location, New Grad/Entry Level, Discipline, Keywords, and International. Women's and college resources include an extensive list of helpful topics for these important groups.

Standard Features:

Cost to see jobs: Free; registration required
Automatic job updates: Yes
Number of jobs: N/A
Specialty/Industry: All
Cost to post resume: Free; registration required
Posting period: 180 days
Geographic coverage: International
Full- or part-time/contract: All

Special Features:

◆ Career resources sections include Resume Services, Career Advice, Salary Information, In The Workplace, and Career Counseling Services.

◆ Career Publications section highlights books and magazines to help job seekers in their career search.

◆ CyberFair,™ a real-time virtual job fair, facilitates private discussion between job seekers and employers.

www.career.com

Career Builder

Career Builder provides a variety of career resources, with a network of over 27 leading career sites. The "Getting Hired" section includes information, tips and answers about all aspects of the job hunting process, from creating a resume, to negotiating offers. "Working Life" helps anyone and everyone balance career and personal lives successfully, from office politics to career transition.

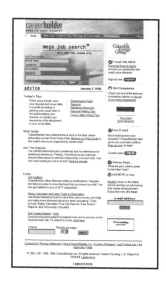

Standard Features:

Cost to see jobs: Free; registration required

Automatic job updates: Yes; via personal search agent

Number of jobs: Over 1,000,000

Specialty/Industry: All; especially sales and hi-tech

Cost to post resume: N/A

Posting period: N/A

Geographic coverage: International

Full- or part-time/contract: All

Special Features:

◆ College & Entry Level, Self-Employed, and Working Women "Communities" provide support and advice on a variety of subtopics.

◆ Daily career tips featuring a variety of hints and tricks to staying happy in your current job or finding a dream job.

◆ Free monthly ACHIEVE e-zine featuring the latest advice and tips on job hunting and career advancement.

www.careerbuilder.com

Career City

Launched in 1995 by Adams Media Corporation, CareerCity's traffic has risen to over 2.5 million page views per month. Look further than your initial glance; CareerCity includes far more than computer and hi-tech careers, in which it specializes. Check out a variety of resources to help you find your dream job!

Standard Features:

Cost to see jobs: Free; registration required

Automatic job updates: Yes

Number of jobs: Over 230,000

Specialty/Industry: All; especially Computer/Hi-Tech Careers

Cost to post resume: Free; registration required; paid options

Posting period: 90 days

Geographic coverage: International

Full- or part-time/contract: All

Special Features:

- ◆ 7,000 Employment Services.
- ◆ 1,000 Temporary Placement Firms.
- ◆ Comprehensive listing of companies with jobs posted online, including brief description of the companies.
- ◆ Virtual job fairs, searchable by city.

www.careercity.com

Career Mosaic

CareerMosaic, one of the most easily navigated sites, started in 1994. It includes a variety of different job "communities," identified by industries such as accounting and finance, health care, human resources, insurance, and technology. Users can take a weekly career poll to learn what other job seekers have to say. Job seekers can search by featured company, job title, or keyword.

Standard Features:

Cost to see jobs: Free; registration required

Automatic job updates: Yes

Number of jobs: Over 100,000

Specialty/Industry: All

Cost to post resume: Free; registration required; paid options

Posting period: 120 days

Geographic coverage: International

Full- or part-time/contract: All

Special Features:

- ◆ Usenet search.
- ◆ Career resource center includes: resume writing, networking, relocation, international gateway, FORTUNE careers, what's hot with job searching, diversity for minorities.
- ◆ Online job fairs.

www.careermosaic.com

CareerPath

CareerPath, co-founded in October 1995 by six major national newspapers, receives most of its job listings from newspapers, though employers also post directly to the site. Companies are searchable by geography, industry, and keyword. Career news, facts and figures, "tales from the trenches" and career tests give job seekers an extra advantage.

Standard Features:

Cost to see jobs: Free; registration required

Automatic job updates: Yes

Number of jobs: Classifieds from 88 nationwide newspapers

Specialty/Industry: All

Cost to post resume: Free; registration required

Posting period: 6 months

Geographic coverage: International

Full- or part-time/contract: All

Special Features:

◆ Live chat events with recruiters and career counselors.

◆ Special contests, such as $50,000 Payday and Win a Work Wardrobe.

◆ Career profile lists more than resume.

◆ Job fairs are searchable by location.

www.careerpath.com

CareerSite

Career Site offers some dynamic career sections for job seekers, including investigation, resumes and cover letters, interviewing (broken into case and informational interviewing), salary negotiation and relocation, and a variety of employment opportunities. With specialized anonymous profiling, you decide to whom you want to release your contact information, and how much you'd like to show!

Standard Features:

Cost to see jobs: Free; registration required

Automatic job updates: Yes

Number of jobs: Over 12,000

Specialty/Industry: All; especially Computer/Hi-Tech Careers

Cost to post resume: Free; registration required; paid options

Posting period: Unlimited; 90 days of no activity is "nudged"

Geographic coverage: International

Full- or part-time/contract: All

Special Features:

◆ Employment opportunities include internships, fellowships, seasonal jobs, volunteering, and international opportunities.

◆ Thesaurus-based search engine offers better results.

◆ Extreme ease of reply and resume storage.

◆ Message center.

www.careersite.com

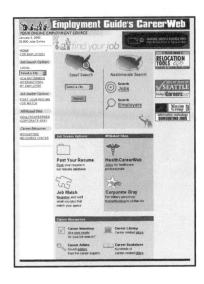

CareerWeb

CareerWeb provides job seekers with the ultimate career library through which you can purchase career books! Online resources include career counseling and skills development, as well as information about internships, relocation, resume preparation, salary negotiation, and reference checking sources. Conduct a city, nationwide, international, or employer-based search for your dream job!

Standard Features:

Cost to see jobs: Free; registration required

Automatic job updates: Yes

Number of jobs: Over 40,000

Specialty/Industry: All

Cost to post resume: Free; registration required

Posting period: 90 days; renewal reminder sent

Geographic coverage: International

Full- or part-time/contract: All

Special Features:

◆ Links to HealthCareerWeb—specialized opportunities for those in the healthcare field, and Corporate Gray Online—specialized job searching for transitioning military personnel.

◆ Links to community job newspapers.

◆ Career inventory includes a readiness inventory so job seekers may determine whether they are doing all they can in their current jobs.

www.careerweb.com

Classifieds2000

At first you may think Classifieds 2000 offers too much... but take a second look and realize that it can provide full coverage of all things job-related... from the car you need to drive to work to the home to which you will relocate! The easy-to-use job search interface includes a wide variety of jobs from classified newspaper ads, and features special employers, start-up companies, and domestic jobs!

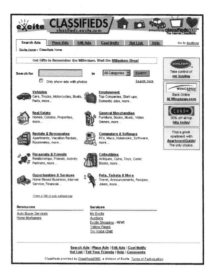

Standard Features:

Cost to see jobs: Free; registration required

Automatic job updates: Yes

Number of jobs: Over 270,000

Specialty/Industry: All

Cost to post resume: Free; registration required; paid options

Posting period: N/A

Geographic coverage: International

Full- or part-time/contract: All

Special Features:

◆ Research industry profiles and advice, including profiles of successful job candidates, when to accept an offer, and telephone interviews.

◆ Career advice section with articles on corporate strategy, personal/career development, job search, and company insights.

◆ Links to special career articles.

www.classifieds2000.com

College Central

Select your entrance into this dynamic site, based on whether you are a student, alumni, employer, or career service provider! Once inside, your customized portal provides a variety of information, including news, weather, stocks, and free email. You can also visit five career experts or a variety of useful links for answers to your educational and employment questions.

Standard Features:

Cost to see jobs: Free; registration required

Automatic job updates: Yes

Number of jobs: 2 million

Specialty/Industry: All

Cost to post resume: Free; registration required

Posting period: N/A

Geographic coverage: International

Full- or part-time/contract: All

Special Features:

- ◆ Specially featured schools offer students and alumni increased resources.
- ◆ Search the 34 largest job sites on the Internet.
- ◆ Bi-weekly career advice e-zine.
- ◆ Extensive list of job and Grad school fairs.

www.collegecentral.com

ConsultLink

Since 1995, ConsultLink, the largest Web directory of consultants and consulting firms, has helped companies locate consultants. Consultants can gain work in three ways: a manager contacts you based on your consulting profile, potential projects are emailed to consultants with matching primary skills and location, or ConsultLink filters responses to announcements for managers.

Standard Features:

Cost to see jobs: Free; registration required

Automatic job updates: N/A

Number of jobs: N/A

Specialty/Industry: All; especially Hi-Tech

Cost to post resume: Free; registration required

Posting period: 90 days

Geographic coverage: International

Full- or part-time/contract: Contract

Special Features:

- ◆ Consultant resources include articles: Facing pressure to go onto a Payroll?, General Liability coverage for Independent Consultants, and discounts for *Contract Professional Magazine*.
- ◆ Links to taxes and regulation, association, and international information.
- ◆ Online bookstore.
- ◆ Sample consulting resumes.

www.consultlink.com

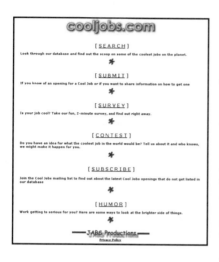

CoolJobs

Is your job cool? Log in to Cool Jobs and take a quick test to find out... can your job match out to exciting careers such as: Yahoo Netsurfer, Hot Air Balloon Ground Crew, Cirque du Soleil Artist, or Jeopardy! Contestant? This site presents you with a database of cool jobs on the net, in categories such as adventure, bodyguard, beer, circus, dude ranch, and Disney jobs.

Standard Features:

Cost to see jobs: Free

Automatic job updates: Yes

Number of jobs: N/A

Specialty/Industry: Cool jobs!

Cost to post resume: N/A

Posting period: N/A

Geographic coverage: International

Full- or part-time/contract: All

Special Features:

◆ Mailing list for new cool jobs not listed in the database.

◆ Contest for "the coolest job in the world" may lead to working in your dream job for 24 hours!

◆ Work humor for when your job search gets too serious: "The Differences Between You And Your Boss," "The Keys To Business Success," "The Performance Review Lexicon," and "Things To Say At a Job Interview."

www.cooljobs.com

DICE

Started in 1994, Dice.com claims to list 10 times the number of IT jobs as its nearest competitor, and it's easy to see that their job numbers are substantial! By filling out a skills profile, job seekers' information is broadcast to 10,000 recruiters and employers. Job seekers often find positions within 48 hours!

Standard Features:

Cost to see jobs: Free; registration required

Automatic job updates: Yes

Number of jobs: Over 160,000

Specialty/Industry: All; especially Hi-Tech Careers

Cost to post resume: Free; registration required; paid options

Posting period: fewer than 30 days

Geographic coverage: International

Full- or part-time/contract: Full-time/contract

Special Features:

◆ Special links to associations & user groups, articles and publications, financial resources, programming resources, and recruiter resources.

◆ Jobs are updated daily.

◆ Metro search lets you search top 20 metro locations, including Atlanta, Chicago, Denver, New York, Raleigh, Seattle, Silicon Valley, Washington, D.C., and Canadian cities.

www.dice.com

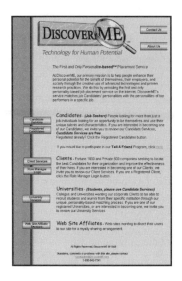

DiscoverME

DiscoverME takes a different approach for job seekers, matching personality traits and background information to the needs of employers. After filling out profile information, you'll receive feedback identifying personality styles and career preferences. The site emails you matches with employers, and offers you the opportunity to approve or decline the match.

Standard Features:

Cost to see jobs: Free; registration required

Automatic job updates: Yes

Number of jobs: N/A

Specialty/Industry: All

Cost to post resume: Free; registration required

Posting period: 12-48 weeks

Geographic coverage: International

Full- or part-time/contract: All

Special Features:

◆ Personal career feedback interprets candidate's profile answers to match work environments (including activity level, organizational structure, flexibility level, and social environment preferences) and work styles (work personality, planning and organizational preferences, preferred work functions, and individual/group settings.

◆ Tell A Friend program entitles you to $250 if your recommended friend becomes placed through the site.

www.discoverme.com

Exec-U-Net

Exec-U-Net provides job, salary, career management and networking organization for executives with salaries in excess of $100,000+. The site provides a career management bookshelf and networking activities for its members, including interactive networking meetings through which members trade leads, insider connections, and job outlook information.

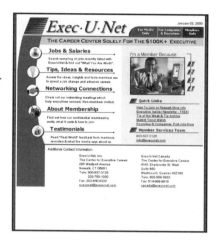

Standard Features:

Cost to see jobs: Free; registration required

Automatic job updates: No

Number of jobs: 20,000

Specialty/Industry: $100,000+ jobs

Cost to post resume: $125-$325

Posting period: 12-48 weeks

Geographic coverage: International

Full- or part-time/contract: All

Special Features:

◆ Three member newsletters: Bi-weekly, electronic *Executive Insider* newsletter provides executive tips and trends; biweekly *Exec-U-Notes* provides job search tactics and strategies; and quarterly *Networds* covers career management trends and strategies.

◆ Members receive free resume review and career coach recommendations.

www.execunet.net

Headhunter.net

Since its appearance in 1996, Headhunter.net has greatly expanded its number of users, claiming 116,000+ visitors per day! Despite the traffic volume, job seekers are easily able to gain an individual feel for their needs, including a wide variety of customized search options. Its simple format should prove easy-to-use for even the newest novice.

Standard Features:

Cost to see jobs: Free; registration required

Automatic job updates: Yes

Number of jobs: Over 230,000

Specialty/Industry: All; especially Computer/Hi-Tech Careers

Cost to post resume: Free; registration required; paid options

Posting period: 90 days before update notice sent

Geographic coverage: International

Full- or part-time/contract: All

Special Features:

♦ Jobseekers may pay to upgrade their resumes' placement.

♦ Numerous privacy options for resume postings enable job seekers to keep their identity confidential.

♦ Comprehensive listing of companies with jobs posted online, including brief description of the companies.

♦ Jobs are under 45 days old.

www.headhunter.net

Hire Ability

This virtual meeting place provides an interactive way for freelance professionals and the companies that need them for specialized projects. Contractors can find opportunities by filling out a profile or searching through the online jobs, which are grouped into several specialties: computing, art, marketing, writing, consulting, and miscellaneous.

Standard Features:

Cost to see jobs: Free; registration required

Automatic job updates: Yes

Number of jobs: 3,000

Specialty/Industry: All

Cost to post resume: Free; registration required

Posting period: 6 months

Geographic coverage: International

Full- or part-time/contract: Contract

Special Features:

◆ Resources section includes programming languages, software reviews, relevant links, industry trends, the history of outsourcing, screening clients, and career development.

◆ Users can "hide" profiles during inactive times.

◆ FAQ for independent contractors covers a wide variety of issues, highlighting the benefits and drawbacks of independent contracting.

www.hireability.com

Homeworkers.com

Dedicated to the homeworker, homeworkers.com provides a wide variety of articles, stories, resources, and jobs. Areas of special focus include: medical transcription, mystery shopping, telecommuting, programming, and writing. At home courses include freelance writing, decorative, basketeering, paralegal, Internet marketing, and many other possibilities.

Standard Features:

Cost to see jobs: Free; registration required

Automatic job updates: No

Number of jobs: Over 47,000

Specialty/Industry: Homeworkers

Cost to post resume: N/A

Posting period: N/A

Geographic coverage: International

Full- or part-time/contract: All

Special Features:

◆ Registration includes free job aptitude test, monthly e-magazine, link to job fairs, and salary information.

◆ Online store includes variety of items for homeworkers, including books, tapes, CDs, transcription devices.

◆ Coaches help lead and maintain special topic channels about which they have knowledge and experience.

www.homeworkers.com

Hot Jobs

HotJobs offers many privacy measures... job seekers can make their resumes available only to those companies to whom they apply or can choose up to 20 companies to block. You can also sign up for a free email account to ensure privacy. No headhunters are allowed, and special career channels include health, human resources, and retail. Job seekers can browse by location, job type, or company.

Standard Features:

Cost to see jobs: Free; registration required

Automatic job updates: Yes

Number of jobs: N/A

Specialty/Industry: All

Cost to post resume: Free; registration required

Posting period: Indefinite

Geographic coverage: National

Full- or part-time/contract: All

Special Features:

◆ Resume statistics area lists number of times resume has come up in searches, how many times it has been viewed, and the number of jobs for which you have applied.

◆ $1,000 to the job seeker with the most inspired letter about how they found a job on our site.

◆ *The Forecast* e-zine highlights relocation, new trends, job forecasts, and campus primer.

www.hotjobs.com

idealist

idealist provides a comprehensive resource not only for people seeking jobs with nonprofit organizations, but also a variety of tools for nonprofits. The jobs include full-time opportunities, internships, consulting (jobs and internships), and much more. You may also subscribe to two daily email newsletters—one provides information about available jobs; the other, internships.

Standard Features:

Cost to see jobs: Free; registration required
Automatic job updates: Yes
Number of jobs: N/A
Specialty/Industry: Nonprofit
Cost to post resume: N/A
Posting period: N/A
Geographic coverage: International
Full- or part-time/contract: All

Special Features:

♦ *Ideas in Action*, email newsletter that provides brief selection of news and pointers to useful nonprofit resources.

♦ Helpful hints for nonprofit job seekers include information about resumes and cover letters, professional associations, awards for nonprofit work, working or volunteering abroad, links to other nonprofit jobs on the Web, and academic programs for nonprofit managers.

www.idealist.org

Job Bank USA

Jobseekers can search for jobs in a variety of categories, including newspapers, newsgroups, international, and industry. Special career building links point to career services, relocation services, work search books, interview tips, resume preparation, and career planning questionnaires. Career fairs and a comprehensive Web search engine also help job seekers find their ideal jobs.

Standard Features:

Cost to see jobs: Free; registration required

Automatic job updates: Yes

Number of jobs: Over 8,000

Specialty/Industry: All

Cost to post resume: Free; registration required

Posting period: 1 year

Geographic coverage: International

Full- or part-time/contract: All

Special Features:

◆ Special career assessment tools include handwriting analysis, psychological type profiles, and stress, sales reluctance, and self-esteem tests.

◆ Resume broadcaster sends your resumes to over 3,400 companies.

◆ Special reference checking tools enable job seekers to determine how their references portray them.

www.jobbankusa.com

Job Options

Formerly E-span, this site has been providing quality resources for job seekers since 1991. Search through a variety of career tools, including employment trends and forecasts, career assessment and evaluation services, and associations. Jobs are searchable by state/province, job category, employers, and keyword. Comprehensive job transitioning services include how to find a new home online.

Standard Features:

Cost to see jobs: Free; registration required
Automatic job updates: Yes
Number of jobs: N/A
Specialty/Industry: All
Cost to post resume: Free; registration required
Posting period: 90 days
Geographic coverage: International
Full- or part-time/contract: All

Special Features:

◆ 10 success stories chosen per month; prizes awarded.

◆ Career management area, co-sponsored by Compuserve, provides online experts and conferences.

◆ Career tools include: writing resumes and letters, business and salary information, special career articles, interviewing resources, career fairs, online continuing education, relocation, and information for working parents.

www.joboptions.com

Jobs Online

This new site, launched in February 1999, provides free services not only to job seekers, but also to employers. Plus, you receive free long distance with your registration! Over 40 fields with 200 links to different salary information sites provide you with comprehensive resources to determine how much you should be earning.

Standard Features:

Cost to see jobs: Free; registration required

Automatic job updates: No; maybe in future

Number of jobs: Over 200,000

Specialty/Industry: All

Cost to post resume: Free; registration required

Posting period: 60 days

Geographic coverage: National

Full- or part-time/contract: All

Special Features:

- ◆ Extensive job aptitude test.
- ◆ Monthly e-zine *JobFACTS*, provides tips and tricks for job searching.
- ◆ Links to career fairs across the country.

www.jobsonline.com

Job Trak

This site targets students and alumni of member schools, resulting in a secure, private community. An online career fair presents "virtual booths" in a variety of categories, such as aerospace-defense, entertainment, and utilities. Career forums include career counseling, internships, job search tips, and career tips for business, finance, entertainment, education, hi-tech, public service, and more!

Standard Features:

Cost to see jobs: Free; registration required

Automatic job updates: No

Number of jobs: Over 400,000

Specialty/Industry: All

Cost to post resume: Free; registration required

Posting period: 90 days

Geographic coverage: International

Full- or part-time/contract: All

Special Features:

◆ "Scholarship Trak" includes scholarship search engine, government programs, loan programs, glossary of terms, and links to other helpful sites.

◆ Job search tips include a career index with descriptions to thousands of jobs, personality tests, city snapshots, and more.

◆ Career contact network of alumni, employers, parents, and students offer advice to job seekers.

www.jobtrak.com

Monster.com

Monster.com currently includes 170,000 jobs and over 30,000 employers. It provides job seekers with a comprehensive jobsearch environment, including career tips, interactive message boards and chat rooms with expert advisors. It also offers different career "zones" that concentrate on specialty areas, such as executive, nonprofit, international, and human resources.

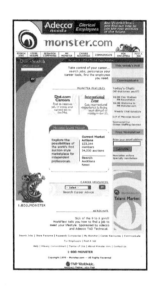

Standard Features:

Cost to see jobs: Free; registration required

Automatic job updates: Yes

Number of jobs: Over 250,000

Specialty/Industry: All; especially Computer/Hi-Tech Careers

Cost to post resume: Free; registration required; paid options

Posting period: 1 year

Geographic coverage: International

Full- or part-time/contract: All

Special Features:

- ◆ Comprehensive resume builder, watchful search agent, and complete tracking system (http://my.monster.com).
- ◆ Career Chat rooms to converse with like-minded job seekers and career experts.
- ◆ New "talent market" for independent contractors.
- ◆ Free email newsletters concerning new developments at Monster.com or information on specific job specialties.

www.monster.com

NationJob

Job seekers can search NationJob's extensive offering of jobs by specifying field/position, location, education, duration of employment, and salary range. NationJob includes a wide variety of special services including a network of specialty. P.J. Scout, the "job pusher" provides subscribers with a weekly list of job descriptions (if over 5 match in a single week) with links to the full text.

Standard Features:

Cost to see jobs: Free; registration required

Automatic job updates: Yes

Number of jobs: Over 10,000

Specialty/Industry: All

Cost to post resume: Free;

Posting period: Indefinite

Geographic coverage: International

Full- or part-time/contract: All

Special Features:

◆ Specialty industries include automotive, higher education, legal, and wireless and cellular.

◆ Custom community sites for employers highlight jobs with their companies and available jobs.

◆ Assessment tests, career counseling, resume critiques, reference checking, relocation information, and company research information help prepare job seekers for an effective search.

www.nationjob.com

Net-Temps

NetTemps specifically targets contract and temporary employment markets, providing a unique resource for job seekers. Specialized career channels include engineering, sales and marketing, and health care. Use the "customized desktop" to access chat rooms, message boards, relocation tools, and over 5,000 recruiters to coach you through the interview and selection process.

Standard Features:

Cost to see jobs: Free; registration required

Automatic job updates: Yes

Number of jobs: N/A

Specialty/Industry: All

Cost to post resume: Free; registration required

Posting period: 30 days

Geographic coverage: International

Full- or part-time/contract: Contract/Temporary

Special Features:

◆ Relocation resources include city comparisons, city guides, COLA, community profiles, real estate information, and rental searches.

◆ *Job Seeker's News*—weekly online newsletter.

◆ Career tips include resources on writing resumes and cover letters, action words list, interviewing, and networking.

---

www.net-temps.com

Overseas Jobs

Claims to be the number one resource for international employment and work abroad. This site works well when viewed with other sites in the AboutJobs.com Network: SummerJobs.com, ResortJobs.com, and Intern-Jobs.com. Search by location or keyword, and if you cannot find the job you seek, check out the links to over 750 overseas career resources in 40 countries.

Standard Features:

Cost to see jobs: Free; registration required

Automatic job updates: N/A

Number of jobs: Several thousand

Specialty/Industry: All

Cost to post resume: N/A

Posting period: N/A

Geographic coverage: International

Full- or part-time/contract: All

Special Features:

- ◆ SummerJobs.com features seasonal and summer job opportunities for students and temporary workers.
- ◆ ResortJobs.com features worldwide resort jobs with ski areas, camps, parks, cruise ships, and hotels.
- ◆ InternJobs.com features a variety of internships.
- ◆ Directory of nearly 4,000 other sites offering job listings, career information and resumes.

www.overseasjobs.com

Real Jobs

This new site features jobs in over forty different categories, including information technology, telecommunications, financial services, health care, marketing, management, retail, media, and more. You can be assured that your identity is private here; Real Jobs uses a protected user name and password, and allows you to prevent unwanted recruiters from viewing your resume.

Standard Features:

Cost to see jobs: Free; registration required

Automatic job updates: No

Number of jobs: Over 200,000

Specialty/Industry: All

Cost to post resume: Free; registration required

Posting period: Indefinite

Geographic coverage: International

Full- or part-time/contract: All

Special Features:

◆ Resume and interview preparation advice.

◆ Online job fairs feature retail, information technology, professional/financial services, and health care "booths."

◆ Browse through information and job listings for featured employers.

◆ 25 Hottest Careers for Women.

www.realjobs.com

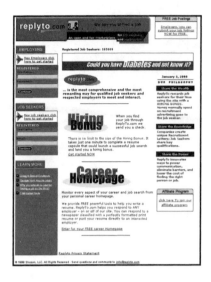

Replyto

Want to earn some money for your job search effort? Visit Replyto, and earn a minimum of $100 as a hiring bonus! Once you create your resume, you can convert it into a professional print or Web page design by choosing from several templates, or you can email or fax it (for a fee) to any employer. You also can display only non-identifying information in your resume.

Standard Features:

Cost to see jobs: Free; registration required

Automatic job updates: Yes

Number of jobs: Classifieds from 88 nationwide newspapers

Specialty/Industry: All

Cost to post resume: Free; registration required

Posting period: 6 months

Geographic coverage: International

Full- or part-time/contract: All

Special Features:

- ◆ Employers are not charged for their job postings.
- ◆ Link to www.10minuteresume.com walks you through the different sections of a resume and provides expert advice on phrases, tips, and action words.
- ◆ Automatic response system enables you to decide which companies should receive your resume.
- ◆ Monitor your resume activity.

www.replyto.com

Top Jobs on the Net

This relatively new site provides an expansive list of international companies looking for top talent. Each country has its own site, searchable by job categories, keywords, or new jobs. After registering, you can immediately search according to your chosen keywords/category, or you may select to have jobs emailed to you.

Standard Features:

Cost to see jobs: Free; registration required

Automatic job updates: Yes

Number of jobs: N/A

Specialty/Industry: All

Cost to post resume: N/A

Posting period: N/A

Geographic coverage: International

Full- or part-time/contract: All

Special Features:

- ◆ TopGrads, an area designed for graduate job seekers, features employers with either graduate training programs or employment opportunities.

- ◆ Career resource section includes career influences and expectations surveys; advice concerning resumes/CVs, interviews, and making the right impression; and *JobMag*.

- ◆ Book reviews and top links to Internet resources.

www.topjobs.com

Transition Assistance Online

This extensive Web site for transitioning service members and veterans provides a plethora of information for this special group, and others! Special career information includes self-assessment, financial planning, job hunting strategies, resume and letter writing tips, interviewing techniques, and relocation considerations.

Standard Features:

Cost to see jobs: Free; registration required

Automatic job updates: Yes

Number of jobs: Over 170,000

Specialty/Industry: All, especially Computer/Hi-Tech Careers

Cost to post resume: Free; registration required; paid options

Posting period: 1 year

Geographic coverage: International

Full- or part-time/contract: All

Special Features:

◆ Entrepreneur center.

◆ Special areas for spouses and dependents.

◆ Continuing education resources.

◆ Search through a variety of fairs and special events.

◆ Skill code translator helps you translate your military code into a civilian title and description.

www.taonline.com

USAJOBS

The Office of Personnel Management has prepared the U.S. Government's official sites for jobs and employment information. This site provides everything from a federal salary and benefits list to veterans and uniformed services information. The wide variety of application options is also invaluable—from Census to NASA!

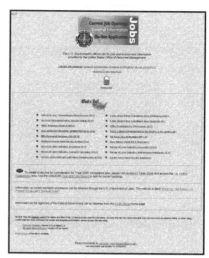

Standard Features:

Cost to see jobs: Free; registration required

Automatic job updates: Yes

Number of jobs: Over 170,000

Specialty/Industry: Federal jobs

Cost to post resume: Free; registration required

Posting period: N/A

Geographic coverage: International

Full- or part-time/contract: All

Special Features:

◆ Optional Application for Federal Employment (OF-612) may be printed in several formats.

◆ Information on Federal job scams includes printable report.

◆ Presidential Management Intern Program and Student Employment.

◆ Extensive information on how to apply for Federal jobs.

www.usajobs.opm.gov

Virtual Resume

This site places the resume, rather than the recruiter, in the spotlight. To protect your identity, you can post a confidential resume, which shows the contents of your resume without your name or other identifying information. Virtual Resume automatically forwards inquiries to your email address and you choose whether to contact the prospective employer.

Standard Features:

Cost to see jobs: Free; registration required
Automatic job updates: No
Number of jobs: 125,000 within 7 days of posting
Specialty/Industry: All
Cost to post resume: Free; registration required
Posting period: 6 months
Geographic coverage: International
Full- or part-time/contract: All

Special Features:

◆ Links to other sites with online resume banks.

◆ Tips and tricks for writing resumes and cover letters, as well as interviewing information and resources.

◆ Download government jobs by state.

◆ Bookstore includes recommended titles and search engine for other titles.

www.virtualresume.com

WashingtonJobs

This newly-revamped site, though centered in the Washington, D.C. area, provides excellent advice and resources no matter where you live! This extremely active site includes weekly, online chat sessions with career experts. Career advice includes tips and taboos on resumes, interviewing, and negotiating salaries, as well as expert advice on work/life issues.

Standard Features:

Cost to see jobs: Free; registration required

Automatic job updates: Yes

Number of jobs: Over 20,000

Specialty/Industry: All; especially Computer/Hi-Tech Careers

Cost to post resume: Free; registration required; paid options

Posting period: 1 year

Geographic coverage: International

Full- or part-time/contract: All

Special Features:

- ◆ Job matrix presents matrix of job types and locations to help you identify your perfect job.
- ◆ Specially featured career sectors help you identify opportunities, key players and companies, professional events, and training.
- ◆ List of recent appointments within the DC area.

www.washingtonjobs.com

5

RESEARCH, RESEARCH, RESEARCH

No matter how you look at it, effective research can help make you one of the best candidates for the job. You already know that learning about the company for which you will work is an essential part of your job search. In Chapter 2, you learned how to research career paths and information associated with specific types of jobs. Here we look at researching companies.

The Internet helps you research in many ways previously unavailable to job seekers. Web sites provide a variety of information on the company's executive officers, financials, and its business principles. This information can help you make an informed career decision about companies which interest you. For example, if you uncover information that a merger is in the works, take care: mergers can often result in downsizing, and new hires may have very little job security. Your searches may reveal that the company has been struggling financially, which may affect your salary and budget.

You can also access news releases related to the company and the industry, as well as forecasts for the industry. Dig a little deeper, and you can uncover information about competitors, customers, or other companies. If you take the knowledge you have gained through your research into an interview, you demonstrate your initiative, well-informed interest in the company, and that you can access resources that may help the company!

If you can't find any or enough information about the company you are researching through a single site listed in this chapter, try the other sites. If that fails, the search engines listed in Chapter 1 may provide the information you seek.

The Better Business Bureau System
www.bbb.org

Phonebook/Directory

Better Business Bureaus (BBBs) "promote and foster the highest ethical relationship between businesses and the public through voluntary self-regulation, consumer and business education, and service excellence." They can prove an excellent way to check out consumer complaints filed against a company in which you are interested.

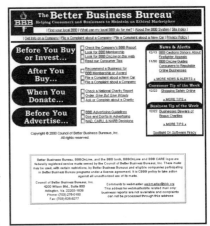

What if you're not interested in customer service? It still affects you—a company without high standards of ethical treatment for its customers probably needs to address internal problems. Those problems may have occurred with only one or two customer service representatives, or the executive level of the company may not be operating in an ethical manner.

In either case, if customers complain to the BBBs about poor quality and/or service, the company may be facing legal or financial battles. It's hard enough to start a new job in a strong, well-established company! These complaints are not definite indicators that you **shouldn't** go to work for a company with bad reports; just be informed about possible problems that divert resources and attention from your salary, program funding, and job performance.

SwitchBoard
Phonebook/Directory
www.switchboard.com

Switchboard also provides a directory search process, but you need to provide a state in which it can look (or look nearby). By entering a name and state, you receive the full name of the business, as well as its street address, phone number, and the Web site address. You also receive a map and directions, PLUS you can select What's Nearby[SM].

What's Nearby[SM] gives you a list of eateries, shopping, entertainment, travel, recreation, health, government offices and other nearby businesses. You can also view a city or state map for the area, and information about the city, including Web sites and books.

BigBook
Phonebook/Directory
www.bigbook.com

BigBook provides a valuable directory service, through which you can search by the location, specialized category, or business name for specific organizations. You can also search by telephone number, which would prove helpful if you don't know the name of the company for which you are searching! This site varies from the search engines presented in chapter one in that it basically serves as an online telephone and address directory.

The search function feeds you with a list of categories in which the business you are interested resides (note: searching just by city and state without identifying an organization results in a LONG list of categories!). Select an appropriate category and you will receive, as available, the full name, street address, phone number, fax, and email address for that company, as well as a map and driving directions.

Intellifact
www.intellifact.com
Company/Industry Research

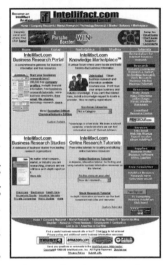

Before you visit any of the other company research sites, check out Intellifact.com for its tutorial, "Business Research on the Internet." The tutorial guides you through six basic steps: on-line research basics, finding company information, following business news, research markets and industries, finding technology information, and exploring other business resources. It also provides a bi-weekly business research newsletter that includes site reviews, product discounts, new search strategies, and more business tools.

The research information provided by this site is also well worth checking out. Over 350,000 company profiles are provided by well-known sites such as Yahoo Financial, Quicken.com, Wright Research Center, Hoover's, and Bloomberg. Market research reports focus on categories including chemicals, electronics, household goods, private companies, and much more. The Knowledge Marketplace™ also provides you with a unique forum through which you can locate and trade business and industry research and knowledge with other users.

Yahoo! Industry News
biz.yahoo.com/industry
Company/Industry Research

Yahoo's special industry information site includes links to a variety of valuable resources through which you can research the companies in which you are interested. Perhaps one of the most valuable sections for the savvy job seeker is the "Related News" section, through which you can find out the hottest, most up-to-date headlines for the organization.

Additional resources include financial information, which provides a profile (business summary, financial summary, officers, stock information, etc.), chart (stock performance), research (stock analysis) and a community message board related to the issues surrounding the company and its stock.

WetFeet
www.wetfeet.com

Company/Industry Research

WetFeet claims to be "the #1 site on the Web to research your job and manage your career," and it's definitely a leader for job seekers! You can start out by perusing a variety of career advice, including special articles by Richard N. Bolles, author of *What Color is Your Parachute?* Free membership entitles you to free downloads, email newsletters, storewide discounts, special offers, and more.

And that's not even touching the company and industry research this site presents. WetFeet offers users access to its Insider Guide series, which provide detailed reports on companies and industries, based on extensive interviews with company insiders and industry experts. The Insider Guides feature company and industry histories, current trends, and insight into the future. WetFeet also provides information about opportunities available in different companies, personnel highlights, key financial statistics, select products and services, and key differentiating factors.

Hoover's Online
www.hoovers.com
Company/Industry Research

Hoover's Handbook 1991: Profiles of Over 500 Major Corporations, led to the origin of Hoover's Online, launched in 1995. This Web site features access to Hoover's company profiles and capsules, as well as business news and other information. The extensive company capsule provides a large amount of free information, such as top competitors, company press releases, news stories, key people, financials, stock charts, and insider trades reports. You can also search the Web for information on the companies you are researching and view contact information, subsidiary locations, and a map to the company.

If you pay extra fees ($14.95 per month or $124.95 per year), you'll be able to access an extensive company history; full officer and competitor lists; products, services, and segment data; real-time SEC filings; and in-depth and historical financials.

Companies Online
www.companiesonline.com
Company/Industry Research

Get ready to delve into some in-depth information about potential employers and the industries in which they exist! CompaniesOnline provides information on over 100,000 public and private companies. You can search by company name, industry, address, ticker symbol, or URL. Once you have completed your search, you'll be presented with a list of Web addresses owned by the company, as well as its DUNS number (and how to order a Dun & Bradstreet report for $20), its ownership information, and its industry. You can revisit the front page and check out the competitors under the industry section.

Dow Jones
www.dowjones.com
Company/Industry Research

Brought to you from the publishers of *The Wall Street Journal,* this site provides you with the latest news about the companies in which you are interested. Searching for the name of the company results in recent articles from Dow Jones business news, relevant sites from Dowjones.com 2000 business Web sites, press release wire releases, articles from *The Wall Street Journal Interactive Edition,* and premium services (free searching and free headlines; $2.95 to view actual articles).

Other categories of interest on the site include: quotes plus lookup, personal finance, forums, lighter side, and many more. You can also research careers, starting a business, and homes and real estate on this site.

Company Sleuth
www.companysleuth.com
Company/Industry Research

This is one of the most comprehensive inside information sites on the Net. When you log in, you can gain instant access to technical trading information, Yahoo! message boards, Raging Bull message boards, and premium information (fee charged). If you want to track companies over time, you can personalize a page with Company Sleuth, and you can also sign up to receive automatic emails on the companies which interest you.

CorporateInformation
www.corporateinformation.com
Company/Industry Research

Corporate Information offers over 15,000 research reports from publicly-traded companies around the world, with in-depth analysis of sales trends, profitability, stock performance, financial position, research and development expenditures, dividends, and much more. Over 20,000 company profiles include a brief description of each company's activities, the names of its top officers, competitor analysis, stock chart, and more. It doesn't stop there. The site also provides a search engine of over 300,000 company profiles and links to over 1,000 other sites that offer corporate information.

GuideStar www.guidestar.org	Company/Industry Research

GuideStar, "the donor's guide to the charitable universe," provides invaluable information about more than 620,000 nonprofit organizations in the United States. You can search for the nonprofit organization in which you are interested by name, subject, state, zip code, or other criteria. The resulting reports include information from the organizations' IRS forms 990, such as assets, income, contact information, chief executive, and board information. Additional information, such as Web sites, company descriptions, and programs/activities, may have been included by the nonprofit organizations, as well.

6

THE INTERVIEW AND NEGOTIATION PROCESSES

You've spent a lot of time so far using the Internet for your job search and have picked out or been approached by employers with jobs that interest you. You've prepared an excellent resume and cover letters tailored to specific employers, then researched industries and organizations so thoroughly that you can recite company financials in your sleep. You've earned the respect you deserve, but don't sit back and relax yet. It's time for the final, and perhaps most grueling, steps in your job search: the interview and negotiation processes.

Power Interviewing

Some people consider interviews to be the most intimidating part in the job search process, but you can actually have fun if you've done your homework. Don't ever go blindly into an interview, whether it be online, over the telephone, or live. It's not worth wasting your time or the employer's, so take some time to properly prepare yourself. Use the tools provided in Chapter 5 to thoroughly research the company with which you are interviewing, and check out some of the following interview books to help you prepare:

- *101 Dynamite Questions to Ask at Your Job Interview* by Richard Fein

- *10 Minute Guide to Job Interviews* by Dana Morgan
- *101 Dynamite Answers to Interview Questions : Sell Your Strengths!* by Caryl Rae and Ronald L. Krannich
- *Winning Interviews for $100,000+ Jobs* by Wendy Enelow

When you get to the interview, shake the interviewer's hand and **be yourself**. At this point, your skills and background have proven that you are an excellent candidate for this company. This is your chance to prove that you are the best possible employee for its needs. Your ability to handle the interview with poise and finesse will reveal that you can handle stressful situations, interact with others in a business environment, and communicate!

Be prepared for multiple interviews, some of which may take place in a group setting. Let the employer(s) start the interview, but don't sit there like a sack of potatoes. Enter into a lively, interactive discussion about why you and the employer need each other. Some of the best ways to communicate your enthusiasm and interest include:

- Prepare some thought-provoking, open-ended questions about the company, department, and the job responsibilities.

- Don't stumble over silence; use it to emphasize moments of thoughtful consideration.

- Provide examples with your answers.

- Identify quantified results that you have achieved.

- Suggest possible solutions you would provide for specific job responsibilities.

- Show that you have researched the company's background by referring to specific media, competitors, or industry issues.

Familiarize yourself with some of the "dangerous" spots you may encounter in an interview situation. Questions about your age, race, religion, disabilities, or marital status are illegal, but are you prepared to alienate the interviewer with the response "you can't ask me that question!" Determine ahead of time how you might turn these question to your advantage. Prepare, also, for questions about your goals, negative experiences with prior supervisors and companies, and your weaknesses. In an interview, anything is fair game!

The following sites will help prepare you for the final steps in your job search:

Job Interview Network   Interviewing
www.job-interview.net

This site provides so many great resources for interviewing, it's difficult to tell where to begin! Try starting with the mock interviews, based on actual job openings—each includes a job description, a practice question set, answer tips, and interview resources. Career-specific interview tips highlight jobs in accounting, aviation, consulting, information technology, marketing, military, religion, teaching, and much more.

Other valuable resources on this great site include an extensive list of reviews for interviewing and career-related books, job interview techniques (including dress, follow-up letters, and the best interview time), advice for behavioral interviews, and illegal questions you may encounter in the interview. If you still haven't been able to find the answer to a tough interview question, you can ask the online experts for help.

Interview Experts
www.interviewexperts.com   Interviewing

Herein you will find a quick and easy navigable guide to interviewing. Not only does it include tough questions, illegal questions, and "the 10 toughest questions job interviewers ask—and how to answer them"; it also provides responses to common career-related questions. The career articles section includes a wide variety of archived news stories from leading writers on interviewing and other career and employment issues. An extensive list of career links features resume writing and posting services, career strategies, college resources, career magazines and readings, search tools, human resources, and much more.

MeetIT (Interview Tips)
www.meetit.com   Interviewing

Although designed for informational technology professionals, the hundreds of free interview tips make this site a true find for anyone preparing for an interview. The interview question section is broken into eight categories that include questions about the applicant, the employer, the work involved, and "tough/negative" issues. Interview tips direct the candidate concerning preparations for the interview, including questions to ask, appearance for the interview, and mistakes made during the interviewing process.

Of course, follow up your interview with a thank you letter to everyone with whom you interviewed. Thank you letters should NOT be sent online, except as a last resort (if the employer is making a decision within 24 hours, email will be a quick attention grabber). If you do send an email thank you letter, make sure you indicate in the email that a hard copy will follow, and follow through!

Salary and Benefit Negotiations

You've done it! The combination of excellent resume, cover letter, job searching and researching, and a superb interview has led to the final phase in the job search process... and the one in which too many people underestimate their value. Few people know what they are really worth, and fail to adequately negotiate salaries and benefits, believing that these options are predetermined and unchangeable. Don't make this tragic mistake. Talk about money and benefits with confidence, because you are VALUABLE to the employer—otherwise, why would they offer you a job?

There are many different considerations to think about at this point, so prepare yourself to help yourself to the salary and benefits you deserve, without appearing greedy. Several books will help get you started:

- *Negotiating Your Salary: How to Make $1,000 a Minute* by Jack Chapman

- *Dynamite Salary Negotiations: Know What You're Worth and Get It!* by Ronald L. and Caryl Rae Krannich, Ph.D.s

Let the employer bring up salary first. If an employer asks you about your salary expectations prior to the offer, either state that you are "flexible," or provide a salary range. If this question is presented prior to the interview (for example, when a recruiter calls you to schedule an interview), it is perfectly acceptable to indicate that you would first like to learn more about the job's responsibilities before you state a salary or range.

The most important step in this process is to **research salary and benefits.** Let's face it, most of us probably don't follow trends for benefits and salary ranges; after all, isn't that a job for human resources professionals? It's time to become your own HR pro, and learn about the salary ranges for the position you seek, in your company, in your industry, in your geographic area.

Think about the "compensation package," which includes not only salary, but also benefits like life, health, and disability insurance; a retirement plan; stock options and profit sharing; and paid leave. If you are moving from one company with a salary of $30,000 per year with no benefits other than paid vacation, into a company that wants to pay you $33,000 per year (a 10% increase in salary), but offers you free health care, life, and disability insurance, as well as an additional five days of paid leave per year, your total compensation package has actually increased more than 10%!

Don't be afraid to ask the employer about the range for your position, as well as for someone with your qualifications. When you learn the range, refrain from leaping with joy or running away! A few moments of silence will indicate that you are considering the offer. If the salary is considerably lower than your research has indicated, mention the range your research discovered—now is the time to uncover the reason for that discrepancy. Also, if applicable, indicate that your training and educational background should place you in the higher end of the range, since you are able to hit the ground running, without extensive training. If you don't seem to be getting anywhere with salary negotiation, approach the possibility of increased benefits, such as more paid vacation, stock options, or a salary review after your probation period has passed.

When you have concluded the negotiations to your satisfaction, pause. Do not accept the position on the spot. Tell the employer you would like the offer in writing and a few days to consider the opportunity. The ball is in your court now, especially once you have a written offer in hand. Return to your online sources to research the information you have been provided. Will you save commuting costs, or will this position involve relocation costs? **Take the time to consider the offer carefully**, and pat yourself on the back for getting the offer!

Impact Publications
www.impactpublications.com
Salary/Interviewing

This site offers the most comprehensive career store you could desire, but it also provides a number of valuable tips that will help in your interviewing and negotiation process. Special interview articles include "What's Your Interview I.Q.?" and "10 Deadly Interview Mistakes Job Seekers Make." Salary negotiation skills include "What's Your Salary I.Q.?" "30 Salary Negotiation Mistakes to Avoid," and "Salary Savvy, Salary Sins."

WageWeb
www.wageweb.com
Salary

WageWeb provides over 160 benchmark positions with compensation data, and its primary purpose is to help recruiters and HR professionals attract and retain new employees. The free data provided includes: title of position, average minimum salary, mean average salary, average maximum salary, and average bonus paid, if any. You can also browse through sample job descriptions and view a sample datasheet that provides a more complete breakdown of the salary and benefits.

Abbott, Langer & Associates
www.abbott-langer.com
Salary

Don't be put off by the heavy focus on report costs on this site; each of the categories has valuable, FREE summary data that can help you with your negotiations. In addition, if the information you seek is not included, you can participate in surveys to gain a 50% discount off the purchase of a report. This site has a variety of different categories, including engineering, marketing/ sales, executive/management, science, nonprofit, accounting, and much more.

American Compensation Association   Salary/Benefits
www.acaonline.org

By selecting "Site Map" and choosing "1999-2000 Salary Budget Survey," you'll gain some difficult to find statistical information about salary growth in relation to inflation. The 1999-2000 survey indicated a steady salary growth between 4.0-4.5% growth for 2000. Survey highlights include the different salary structure increase between nonexempt hourly nonunion employees, nonexempt salaried employees, exempt salaried employees, and officers and executives. In addition, you can also gain information about stock option plans being offered. And that's not all—this site truly provides the latest information on benefits and salary issues. In its newsroom, check out current compensation and benefits news and information, listing and links to HR-related bills pending in the house and senate, and government updates.

National Compensation Survey   Salary
www.bls.gov/comhome.htm

and

National Benefits Survey   Benefits
www.bls.gov/ebshome.htm

The Bureau of Labor Statistics provides both sites, which contain some of the most highly requested data for compensation and benefits. The sites include data up to 1997, which can still be helpful as a baseline. Both list links to *The Compensation and Working Conditions* and *The Monthly Labor Review* publications.

The National Compensation Survey lists specialty industry surveys, occupational wages in the United States, a glossary of compensation terms, a business information guide, and guidelines for evaluating your organization's pay. Other related information includes employment cost trends, occupational employment statistics, a link to the *Occupational Outlook Handbook* (which includes job outlook and earnings), and much more.

The Employee Benefits Survey site breaks down its data into medium and large private establishments and small private establishments. It also includes a variety of current and historical articles arranged by benefit topic and links to additional information.

Employee Benefits Research Institute
www.ebri.org
Benefits

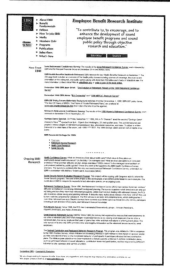

This is **the** source for research conducted on employee benefits! The major research findings listed for 1999 include retirement income (retirement plan design, small employers, savings behavior, etc.), health care (coverage, plan design, public opinion, quality of health care, and long-term care insurance), and social security, all of which can help you not only determine your needs for your current job offer, but also plan well into your retirement.

Additional information includes the Retirement Confidence Survey, which tracks American workers' attitudes and behavior concerning retirement savings and planning; the Defined Contribution and Participant Behavior Research Program, which includes defined contribution plans, such as participant behavior in asset allocations, contribution levels and participation, and response to participant behavior by plan sponsors and service providers. You could easily spend a few hours perusing the fact sheets, testimonies, issue briefs, and notes sprinkled throughout this site!

BenefitsLink   Benefits
www.benefitslink.com

Between the message board, relevant links, newsletter, and Q&A columns, you should be able to find an answer to any question you have about employee benefits, and if you can't find it, you can ask the experts! The BenefitsLink newsletter is archived on the site, and you can also subscribe to receive it via email. The Q&A columns include information by experts, such as 401(K) Plans, COBRA, Commuter Benefits, Eldercare, Taxability of Long Term Care Insurance Ben-

efits, 2000 Monthly Transit and Parking Benefit Limits, and so much more. The employee benefits links cover everything from church plans and bankruptcy to COBRA and stock options.

Employee Relocation Council   Relocation
www.erc.org

While most of this site is most helpful to relocating professionals, it's definitely worth perusing! This comprehensive resource covers the latest relocation trends and industry publications concerning the effective relocation of employees worldwide, and is extremely helpful in its 1999 New Hire Survey. Statistics include information about entry-level/new college graduate, mid-level management/technical, and executive-level positions and the relocation benefits offered to these three groups. Relocation benefits include en route expenses, home-finding trips, temporary living, purchase closing costs, home-marketing assistance, spouse employment assistance, and much more. If you're trying to determine what relocation benefits you require, this will leave no stone unturned!

Virtual Relocation
www.virtualrelocation.com
Relocation

If you are need to figure out actual costs and resources for the different relocation aspects required by your new job, this site provides a comprehensive list to links in the area you are researching! Categories include real estate (firms and agents, property or rental search), parenting (child care, camps), schools (colleges, financial aid), professional (legal resources, health care, financial resources), reference (taxes, government, maps), moving and storage, insurance, and local information (arts and entertainment, sports and recreation, weather forecast), and MUCH more! You can also look up the top 50 cities, take a virtual city tour, meet with the "relocation therapist," and conduct a cost of living analysis. This is definitely helpful when you're making your final decision and starting plans on your move!

ABOUT THE AUTHOR

Kristina Ackley works as electronic PR manager for Network Solutions, Inc., "the dot com people™." She also owns and operates Gryphon Communications, a public relations and Web site design firm located in Manassas, VA.

As a career specialist, she has recruited and selected personnel for numerous organizations, as well as assisted friends and colleagues in their job search. Ackley also has edited a variety of career materials and worked as director of public relations and marketing with Impact Publications, one of the nation's largest career resource centers (Manassas Park, VA).

Ackley regularly writes an online help column for *The Tattling Turtle*, published bi-monthly by the Delta Zeta Northern Virginia Alumnae Association. She was a founding member of Women Halting Online Abuse (WHOA), and continues to participate in that organization, as well as the National Association of Female Executives.

Ackley resides in a suburb of Washington, D.C. She holds a master's degree in Public Relations Management from The University of Maryland at College Park and a bachelor's degree in English from Wittenberg University in Springfield, OH.

Appendix
100+ Internet Job Sites

With the job economy producing new opportunities on a constant basis, it is important for the savvy job seeker to move to the next level. This level includes the Internet as a powerful job search engine, through which you can quickly catapult your career into success. The following sites were featured as the top 100 in this book, or appeared as additional resources. They are categorized according to site focus and alphabetized within their categories.

This list does not seek to show all of the resume and job posting sites online; it merely establishes the top sites from which job seekers can pick and choose how they would like to proceed with their job search. Hundreds of other sites are in existence for every conceivable occupation and region of the world.

Benefits
BenefitsLink .... www.benefitslink.com
Employee Benefits Research Institute .... www.ebri.org
National Benefits Survey .... www.bls.gov/ebshome.htm

Career Profiles
JobProfiles .... www.jobprofiles.com
Occupational Outlook Handbook .... states.bls.gov/ocohome.htm

Company/Industry Research
Companies Online .... www.companiesonline.com
Company Sleuth .... www.companysleuth.com

CorporateInformation .... www.corporateinformation.com
Dow Jones .... www.dowjones.com
GuideStar .... www.guidestar.org
Hoover's Online .... www.hoovers.com
Intellifact .... www.intellifact.com
WetFeet .... www.wetfeet.com
Yahoo! Industry News .... biz.yahoo.com/industry

Counseling Associations

American Counseling Association .... www.counseling.org
International Association of Career Management Professionals .. www.iacmp.org
National Board for Certified Counselors, Inc. .... www.nbcc.org
National Career Networking Association .... www.ncna.com

Interviewing

Interview Experts .... www.interviewexperts.com
Job Interview Network .... www.job-interview.net
MEETIT .... www.meetit.com

Listserv Directories

Egroups .... www.egroups.com
Liszt .... www.liszt.com

Newsgroup Information

DejaNews .... www.dejanews.com
Liszt Newsgroups .... www.liszt.com/news
news.newusers.questions .... www.xs4all.nl/~wijnands/nnq/grouplists.html

Online Abuse Resources

Coalition Against Unsolicited Commercial Email .... www.cauce.org
CyberAngels .... www.cyberangels.org
Women Halting Online Abuse .... www.haltabuse.org

Online Tutorials

CompUSA .... www.compusa.com
Learn the Net .... www.learnthenet.com
Learn2 .... www.learn2.com
Smart Planet .... www.smartplanet.com
Training on the Web .... www.trainingontheweb.net

Phonebooks/Directories

BigBook .... www.bigbook.com
SwitchBoard .... www.switchboard.com
The Better Business Bureau System .... www.bbb.org

Professional Organizations

American Society of Association Executives .... www.asaenet.org
Independent Sector .... www.independentsector.org
Institute of Management Consultants .... www.imcusa.org
National Council of Nonprofit Associations .... www.ncna.org
U.S. Chamber of Commerce .... www.uschamber.org
Women Work! .... www.womenwork.org

Relocation

Employee Relocation Council .... www.erc.org
Virtual Relocation .... www.virtualrelocation.com

Resumes and Cover Letters

4resumes www.4resumes.com
JobStar California .... www.jobstar.org
Knock 'Em Dead .... www.knockemdead.com
ProvenResumes.com .... www.provenresumes.com
Resumania .... www.resumania.com

Resume Posting/Job Listing Sites

4work... www.4work.com
America's Job Bank .... www.ajb.dni.us
Best Jobs USA .... www.bestjobsusa.com
BrilliantPeople.com .... www.brilliantpeople.com
Career Builder.. www.careerbuilder.com
Career City.. www.careercity.com
Career Dot Com .... www.career.com
Career Mosaic .... www.careermosaic.com
CareerPath .... www.careerpath.com
CareerSite .... www.careersite.com
CareerWeb .... www.careerweb.com
Classifieds2000 .... www.classfieds2000.com
College Central .... www.collegecentral.com
ConsultLink .... www.consultlink.com
CoolJobs .... www.cooljobs.com
DICE .... www.dice.com
DiscoverME .... www.discoverme.com
Exec-U-Net .... www.execunet.com
Headhunter.net .... www.headhunter.net
Hire Ability .... www.hireability.com
Homeworkers.com .... www.homeworkers.com
Hot Jobs .... www.hotjobs.com
idealist .... www.idealist.org
Intern Jobs .... www.internjobs.com
Job Bank USA .... www.jobbankusa.com

Job Options .... www.joboptions.com
Job Trak .... www.jobtrak.com
Jobs Online .... www.jobsonline.com
Monster.com .... www.monster.com
NationJob .... www.nationjob.com
Net-Temps .... www.net-temps.com
Overseas Jobs .... www.overseasjobs.com
Real Jobs .... www.realjobs.com
Replyto .... www.replyto.com
Resort Jobs .... www.resortjobs.com
Summer Jobs .... www.summerjobs.com
Top Jobs on the Net .... www.topjobs.com
Transition Assistance Online .... www.taonline.com
USAJOBS .... www.usajobs.opm.gov
Virtual Resume .... www.virtualresume.com
WashingtonJobs .... www.washingtonjobs.com

Salary/Interviewing

Impact Publications .... www.impactpublications.com

Salary

Abbott, Langer & Associates .... www.abbott-langer.com
American Compensation Association .... www.acaonline.org
National Compensation Survey .... www.bls.gov/comhome.htm
WageWeb .... www.wageweb.com

Search Engines

About.com .... www.about.com
All The Web .... www.alltheweb.com
AltaVista .... www.altavista.com
Ask Jeeves .... www.ask.com
DogPile .... www.dogpile.com
Excite .... www.excite.com
Go2Net www.go2net.com
HotBot .... www.hotbot.com
Infoseek .... www.infoseek.com
Lycos .... www.lycos.com
Northern Light .... www.northernlight.com
Snap .... www.snap.com
WebCrawler .... www.webcrawler.com
Webopedia .... webopedia.internet.com
Yahoo .... www.yahoo.com

Self-Assessment

Virus Protection

Etcetera

CAREER RESOURCES

Contact Impact Publications for a free annotated listing of resources or visit the World Wide Web for a complete listing of resources: www.impactpublications.com. The following books are available directly from Impact Publications. Complete the following form or list the titles, include postage (see formula at the end), enclose payment, and send your order to:

IMPACT PUBLICATIONS
9104 Manassas Drive, Suite N
Manassas Park, VA 20111-5211
Tel 1-800/361-1055, 703/361-7300, or Fax 703/335-9486
Quick and easy online ordering: *www.impactpublications.com*

Qty.	Titles	Price	Total
INTERNET JOB SEARCH/HIRING			
	100 Top Internet Job Sites	12.95	
	The Best 100 Web Sites for HR Professionals	13.95	
	Career Exploration On the Internet	15.95	
	Electronic Resumes	19.95	
	Employer's Guide to Recruiting on the Internet	24.95	
	Guide to Internet Job Searching	14.95	
	Heart & Soul Internet Job Search	16.95	
	Internet Resumes	14.95	
	Job Searching Online for Dummies	24.99	
	Resumes in Cyberspace	14.95	
ALTERNATIVE JOBS & EMPLOYERS			
	100 Great Jobs and How To Get Them	17.95	
	101 Careers	16.95	
	Adams Job Almanac 2000	16.95	
	Back Door Guide to Short-Term Job Adventures	21.95	
	Best Jobs for the 21st Century	19.95	
	Careers in Computers	17.95	
	Careers in Health Care	17.95	
	Careers in High Tech	17.95	
	Cool Careers for Dummies	16.99	
	Cybercareers	24.95	
	Directory of Executive Recruiters 2000	47.95	
	Great Jobs Ahead	11.95	
	Health Care Job Explosion!	17.95	
	Hidden Job Market 2000	18.95	
	JobBank Guide to Computer and High-Tech Companies	17.95	
	Media Companies 2000	18.95	
	Sunshine Jobs	16.95	
	Top 2,500 Employers 2000	18.95	
	What Employers Really Want	14.95	
	You Can't Play the Game If You Don't Know the Rules	14.95	

Qty.	Titles	Price	Total

RECRUITERS/EMPLOYERS

	Adams Executive Recruiters Almanac	16.95	
	Directory of Executive Recruiters	47.95	
	Employer's Guide to Recruiting on the Internet	24.95	
	Job Seekers Guide to Executive Recruiters	34.95	
	Job Seekers Guide to Recruiters In. . .Series	36.95	

JOB STRATEGIES AND TACTICS

	101 Ways to Power Up Your Job Search	12.95	
	Career Bounce-Back	14.95	
	Career Chase	17.95	
	Career Intelligence	15.95	
	Career Starter	10.95	
	Complete Idiot's Guide to Changing Careers	17.95	
	Executive Job Search Strategies	16.95	
	Five Secrets to Finding a Job	12.95	
	Get a Job You Love!	19.95	
	Get It Together By 30	14.95	
	Get the Job You Want Series	37.95	
	Get Ahead! Stay Ahead!	12.95	
	Great Jobs for Liberal Arts Majors	11.95	
	How to Get a Job in 90 Days or Less	12.95	
	How to Get Interviews from Classified Job Ads	14.95	
	How to Succeed Without a Career Path	13.95	
	How to Get the Job You Really Want	9.95	
	Is It Too Late To Run Away and Join the Circus?	14.95	
	Job Hunting in the 21st Century	17.95	
	Job Hunting for the Utterly Confused	14.95	
	Knock 'Em Dead 2000	12.95	
	Me, Myself, and I, Inc.	17.95	
	New Rights of Passage	29.95	
	No One Is Unemployable	29.95	
	Part-Time Careers	10.95	
	Perfect Job Search	12.95	
	Perfect Pitch	13.99	
	Portable Executive	12.00	
	Professional's Job Finder	18.95	
	Resumes Don't Get Jobs	10.95	
	So What If I'm 50	12.95	
	Staying in Demand	12.95	
	Strategic Job Jumping	13.00	
	Take Yourself to the Top	13.99	
	Temping: The Insiders Guide	14.95	
	Top 10 Career Strategies for the Year 2000 & Beyond	12.00	
	Top 10 Fears of Job Seekers	12.00	
	VGMs Career Checklist	9.95	
	Welcome to the Real World	13.00	
	What Do I Say Next?	14.00	
	What Employers Really Want	14.95	
	When Do I Start	11.95	
	Who Says There Are No Jobs Out There	12.95	
	Work Happy Live Healthy	14.95	
	Work This Way	14.95	
	You and Co., Inc.	22.00	

TESTING AND ASSESSMENT

| | Career Exploration Inventory | 34.95 | |
| | Career Satisfaction and Success | 14.95 | |

Qty.	Titles	Price	Total
_____	Career Tests	12.95	_____
_____	Dictionary of Holland Occupational Codes	47.00	_____
_____	Discover the Best Jobs For You	14.95	_____
_____	Discover What You're Best At	13.00	_____
_____	Gifts Differing	16.95	_____
_____	Have You Got What It Takes?	12.95	_____
_____	How to Find the Work You Love	10.95	_____
_____	Making Vocational Choices	31.00	_____
_____	New Quick Job Hunting Map	4.95	_____
_____	P.I.E. Method for Career Success	14.95	_____
_____	Putting Your Talent to Work	12.95	_____
_____	Real People, Real Jobs	15.95	_____
_____	Starting Out, Starting Over	14.95	_____
_____	Test Your IQ	6.95	_____
_____	Three Boxes of Life	18.95	_____
_____	Type Talk	11.95	_____
_____	WORKTypes	12.99	_____

INSPIRATION & EMPOWERMENT

Qty.	Titles	Price	Total
_____	Do What You Love, the Money Will Follow	11.95	_____
_____	If Life Is A Game, These Are the Rules	15.00	_____
_____	Love Your Work and Success Will Follow	12.95	_____
_____	Power of Purpose	20.00	_____
_____	Seven Habits of Highly Effective People	14.00	_____
_____	To Build the Life You Want, Create the Work You Love	10.95	_____

RESUMES & LETTERS

Qty.	Titles	Price	Total
_____	$110,000 Resume	16.95	_____
_____	100 Winning Resumes for $100,000+ Jobs	24.95	_____
_____	101 Best Resumes	10.95	_____
_____	101 More Best Resumes	11.95	_____
_____	101 Quick Tips for a Dynamite Resume	13.95	_____
_____	1500+ Key Words for 100,000+	14.95	_____
_____	175 High-Impact Resumes	10.95	_____
_____	Adams Resume Almanac/Disk	19.95	_____
_____	America's Top Resumes for America's Top Jobs	19.95	_____
_____	Asher's Bible of Executive Resumes	29.95	_____
_____	Best Resumes for $75,000+ Executive Jobs	14.95	_____
_____	Blue Collar and Beyond	11.95	_____
_____	Blue Collar Resumes	11.99	_____
_____	Building a Great Resume	15.00	_____
_____	Complete Idiot's Guide to Writing the Perfect Resume	16.95	_____
_____	Cyberspace Resume Kit	16.95	_____
_____	Dynamite Resumes	14.95	_____
_____	Edge Resume and Job Search Strategy	23.95	_____
_____	Electronic Resumes and Online Networking	13.99	_____
_____	Encyclopedia of Job-Winning Resumes	16.95	_____
_____	Gallery of Best Resumes	16.95	_____
_____	Gallery of Best Resumes for Two-Year Degree Graduates	16.95	_____
_____	Heart & Soul Resumes	15.95	_____
_____	High Impact Resumes and Letters	19.95	_____
_____	How to Prepare Your Curriculum Vitae	14.95	_____
_____	Just Resumes	11.95	_____
_____	New Perfect Resume	10.95	_____
_____	Overnight Resume	12.95	_____
_____	Portfolio Power	14.95	_____
_____	Power Resumes	14.95	_____
_____	Quick Resume and Cover Letter Book	12.95	_____
_____	Ready-To-Go Resumes	29.95	_____

Qty.	Titles	Price	Total
_____	Resume Catalog	15.95	_____
_____	Resume Magic	18.95	_____
_____	Resume Power	12.95	_____
_____	Resume Pro	24.95	_____
_____	Resume Shortcuts	14.95	_____
_____	Resumes for the Over-50 Job Hunter	14.95	_____
_____	Resumes for Re-Entry	10.95	_____
_____	Resume Winners from the Pros	17.95	_____
_____	Resumes for Dummies	12.99	_____
_____	Resumes That Knock 'Em Dead	10.95	_____
_____	Savvy Resume Writer	12.95	_____
_____	Sure-Hire Resumes	14.95	_____

COVER LETTERS

Qty.	Titles	Price	Total
_____	101 Best Cover Letters	11.95	_____
_____	175 High-Impact Cover Letters	10.95	_____
_____	201 Winning Cover Letters for the $100,000+ Jobs	24.95	_____
_____	201 Dynamite Job Search Letters	19.95	_____
_____	201 Killer Cover Letters	16.95	_____
_____	Complete Idiot's Guide to the Perfect Cover Letters	14.95	_____
_____	Cover Letters, Cover Letters, Cover Letters	9.99	_____
_____	Cover Letters for Dummies	12.99	_____
_____	Cover Letters that Knock 'Em Dead	10.95	_____
_____	Dynamite Cover Letters	14.95	_____
_____	Gallery of Best Cover Letters	18.95	_____
_____	Haldane's Best Cover Letters for Professionals	15.95	_____
_____	Perfect Cover Letter	10.95	_____

ETIQUETTE AND IMAGE

Qty.	Titles	Price	Total
_____	Business Etiquette and Professionalism	10.95	_____
_____	Dressing Smart in the New Millennium	15.95	_____
_____	Executive Etiquette in the New Workplace	14.95	_____
_____	First Five Minutes	14.95	_____
_____	John Molloy's Dress for Success (For Men)	13.99	_____
_____	New Professional Image	12.95	_____
_____	New Women's Dress for Success	12.99	_____
_____	Red Socks Don't Work	14.95	_____
_____	VGMs Complete Guide to Career Etiquette	12.95	_____
_____	Winning Image	17.95	_____
_____	You've Only Got 3 Seconds	22.95	_____

INTERVIEWING: JOBSEEKERS

Qty.	Titles	Price	Total
_____	101 Dynamite Answers to Interview Questions	12.95	_____
_____	101 Dynamite Questions to Ask at Your Job Interview	14.95	_____
_____	111 Dynamite Ways to Ace Your Job Interview	13.95	_____
_____	Complete Q & A Job Interview Book	14.95	_____
_____	Conquer Interview Objections	10.95	_____
_____	Haldane's Best Answers to Tough Interview Questions	15.95	_____
_____	Information Interviewing	10.95	_____
_____	Interview for Success	15.95	_____
_____	Interview Strategies ThatWill Get You the Job You Want	12.99	_____
_____	Interview Power	12.95	_____
_____	Job Interviews for Dummies	12.99	_____
_____	Killer Interviews	10.95	_____
_____	Savvy Interviewer	10.95	_____
_____	Successful Interviewing for College Seniors	11.95	_____
_____	Sweaty Palms	8.95	_____

Qty.	Titles	Price	Total

NETWORKING

Qty.	Titles	Price	Total
_____	52 Ways to Re-Connect, Follow Up, and Stay in Touch	14.95	_____
_____	Dig Your Well Before You're Thirsty	24.95	_____
_____	Dynamite Networking for Dynamite Jobs	15.95	_____
_____	Dynamite Tele-Search	12.95	_____
_____	Effective Networking	10.95	_____
_____	Golden Rule of Schmoozing	12.95	_____
_____	Great Connections	19.95	_____
_____	How to Work a Room	11.99	_____
_____	Networking for Everyone	16.95	_____
_____	People Power	14.95	_____
_____	Power Networking	14.95	_____
_____	Power Schmoozing	12.95	_____
_____	Power To Get In	24.95	_____

SALARY NEGOTIATIONS

Qty.	Titles	Price	Total
_____	Dynamite Salary Negotiations	15.95	_____
_____	Get a Raise in 7 Days	14.95	_____
_____	Get More Money on Your Next Job	14.95	_____
_____	Negotiate Your Job Offer	14.95	_____

☞ **SUBTOTAL** $ _____

☞ Virginia residents add 4½% sales tax) _____

☞ Shipping/handling, Continental U.S., $5.00 + _____ $5.00
plus following percentages when **SUBTOTAL** is:

☐ $30-$100—multiply SUBTOTAL by 8% _____

☐ $100-$999—multiply SUBTOTAL by 7% _____

☐ $1,000-$4,999—multiply SUBTOTAL by 6% _____

☐ Over $5,000—multiply SUBTOTAL by 5% _____

☞ ☐ If shipped outside Continental US, add another 5% _____

☞ **TOTAL ENCLOSED** $ _____

SHIP TO: (street address only for UPS or RPS delivery)

Name _____

Address _____

_____

_____

Telephone _____

I enclose ☐ Check ☐ Money Order in the amount of: $ _____

Charge $_____ to ☐ Visa ☐ MC ☐ Discover ☐ AmEx

Card #_____ Exp: _____ / _____

Signature _____

DISCOVER HUNDREDS OF ADDITIONAL RESOURCES ON THE WORLD WIDE WEB!

Looking for the newest and best books, directories, newsletters, wall charts, training programs, videos, computer software, and kits to help you land a job, negotiate a higher salary, or start your own business? Want to learn the most effective way to find a job in Asia or relocate to San Francisco? Are you curious about how to find a job 24 hours a day using the Internet or about what you'll be doing five years from now? Are you trying to keep up-to-date on the latest career resources, but are not able to find the latest catalogs, brochures, or newsletters on today's "best of the best" resources?

Welcome to the first virtual career bookstore on the Internet. Now you're only a click away with Impact Publications' electronic solution to the resource challenge. Visit this rich site to quickly discover everything you ever wanted to know about finding jobs, changing careers, and starting your own business—including many useful resources that are difficult to find in local bookstores and libraries. The site also includes what's new and hot, tips for job search success, and monthly specials. Check it out today!

www.impactpublications.com